Get Ready!

FOR STANDARDIZED TESTS

READING, GRADE TWO

Other Books in the *Get Ready!* Series:

Get Ready! for Standardized Tests: Grade 1 by Joseph Harris, Ph.D.

Get Ready! for Standardized Tests: Grade 2 by Joseph Harris, Ph. D.

Get Ready! for Standardized Tests: Grade 3 by Karen Mersky, Ph.D.

Get Ready! for Standardized Tests: Grade 4 by Joseph Harris, Ph.D.

Get Ready! for Standardized Tests: Grade 5 by Leslie E. Talbott, Ph.D.

Get Ready! for Standardized Tests: Grade 6 by Shirley Vickery, Ph.D.

Get Ready! for Standardized Tests: Math, Grade 1 by Sandy McConnell

Get Ready! for Standardized Tests: Math, Grade 2 by Kristin Swanson

Get Ready! for Standardized Tests: Math, Grade 3 by Susan Osborne

Get Ready! for Standardized Tests: Math, Grade 4 by June Heller

Get Ready! for Standardized Tests: Reading, Grade 1 by Molly Maack

Get Ready! for Standardized Tests: Reading, Grade 3 by Joanne Baker

Get Ready! for Standardized Tests: Reading, Grade 4 by Kris Callahan

Get Ready!

FOR STANDARDIZED TESTS

READING, GRADE TWO

Louise Ulrich

Carol Turkington
Series Editor

McGraw-Hill

New York   Chicago   San Francisco
Lisbon   London   Madrid   Mexico City
Milan   New Delhi   San Juan   Seoul
Singapore   Sydney   Toronto

To my parents, who instilled in me patience, enthusiasm, and the genuine love of teaching, with thanks for everything you have done.

Louise Ulrich

Library of Congress Cataloging-in-Publication Data

Get ready! for standardized tests. Reading.
  p. cm.—(Test preparation series)
  Contents:—[v. 2] Grade two / Louise Ulrich—[v. 3] Grade three / Joanne Baker—[v. 4] Grade four / Kris Callahan.
  ISBN 0-07-137406-X (pbk. : v. 2)—ISBN 0-07-137407-8 (pbk. : v. 3)—ISBN 0-07-137408-6 (pbk. : v. 4)
  1. Achievement tests—United States—Study guides. 2. Reading (Elementary)—United States—Evaluation. 3. Reading (Elementary)—Parent participation—United States. I. Ulrich, Louise. II. Test preparation series (McGraw-Hill Companies)

  LB3060.22 .G48   2001
  372.126'2—dc21   2001030896

McGraw-Hill

A Division of The **McGraw·Hill** Companies

1 2 3 4 5 6 7 8 9 0 COU/COU 0 9 8 7 6 5 4 3 2 1

ISBN 0-07-137406-X

This book was set in New Century Schoolbook by Inkwell Publishing Services.

Printed and bound by Courier.

McGraw-Hill books are available at special quantity discounts to use as premiums and sales promotions, or for use in corporate training programs. For more information, please write to the Director of Special Sales, McGraw-Hill, Professional Publishing, Two Penn Plaza, New York, NY 10121-2298. Or contact your local bookstore.

Contents

SKILLS CHECKLIST

MY CHILD ...	HAS LEARNED	IS WORKING ON
WORD MEANINGS		
PICTURE VOCABULARY		
WORD MEANINGS IN CONTEXT		
ANTONYMS		
SYNONYMS		
HOMOPHONES AND HOMONYMS		
BEGINNING WORD SOUNDS		
ENDING WORD SOUNDS		
CONSONANT BLENDS		
VOWEL SOUNDS		
WORD RECOGNITION		
COMPOUND WORDS		
CONTRACTIONS		
SPELLING		
ROOT WORDS		
SUFFIXES		
PREFIXES		
CAPITALIZATION		
PUNCTUATION		
PARTS OF SPEECH		
SENTENCES		
MAIN IDEA		
SEQUENCE		
CHARACTERS AND SETTINGS		
READING COMPREHENSION		
FACT VS. OPINION		
REALITY VS. FANTASY		
BIOGRAPHY		
POETRY		

Introduction

Almost all of us have taken standardized tests in school. We spent several days bubbling-in answers, shifting in our seats. No one ever told us why we took the tests or what they would do with the results. We just took them and never heard about them again.

Today many parents aren't aware they are entitled to see their children's permanent records and, at a reasonable cost, to obtain copies of any information not protected by copyright, including testing scores. Late in the school year, most parents receive standardized test results with confusing bar charts and detailed explanations of scores that few people seem to understand.

In response to a series of negative reports on the state of education in this country, Americans have begun to demand that something be done to improve our schools. We have come to expect higher levels of accountability as schools face the competing pressures of rising educational expectations and declining school budgets. High-stakes standardized tests are rapidly becoming the main tool of accountability for students, teachers, and school administrators. If students' test scores don't continually rise, teachers and principals face the potential loss of school funding and, ultimately, their jobs. Summer school and private after-school tutorial program enrollments are swelling with students who have not met score standards or who, everyone agrees, could score higher.

While there is a great deal of controversy about whether it is appropriate for schools to use standardized tests to make major decisions about individual students, it appears likely that standardized tests are here to stay. They will be used to evaluate students, teachers, and the schools; schools are sure to continue to use students' test scores to demonstrate their accountability to the community.

The purposes of this guide are to acquaint you with the types of standardized tests your children may take; to help you understand the test results; and to help you work with your children in skill areas that are measured by standardized tests so they can perform as well as possible.

Types of Standardized Tests

The two major types of group standardized tests are *criterion-referenced tests* and *norm-referenced tests*. Think back to when you learned to tie your shoes. First Mom or Dad showed you how to loosen the laces on your shoe so that you could insert your foot; then they showed you how to tighten the laces—but not too tight. They showed you how to make bows and how to tie a knot. All the steps we just described constitute what is called a *skills hierarchy:* a list of skills from easiest to most difficult that are related to some goal, such as tying a shoelace.

Criterion-referenced tests are designed to determine at what level students are performing on various skills hierarchies. These tests assume that development of skills follows a sequence of steps. For example, if you were teaching shoelace tying, the skills hierarchy might appear this way:

1. Loosen laces.
2. Insert foot.
3. Tighten laces.
4. Make loops with both lace ends.
5. Tie a square knot.

Criterion-referenced tests try to identify how far along the skills hierarchy the student has progressed. There is no comparison against anyone else's score, only against an expected skill level. The main question criterion-referenced tests ask is: "Where is this child in the development of this group of skills?"

Norm-referenced tests, in contrast, are typically constructed to compare children in their abilities as to different skills areas. Although the experts who design test items may be aware of skills hierarchies, they are more concerned with how much of some skill the child has mastered, rather than at what level on the skills hierarchy the child is.

Ideally, the questions on these tests range from very easy items to those that are impossibly difficult. The essential feature of norm-referenced tests is that scores on these measures can be compared to scores of children in similar groups. They answer this question: "How does the child compare with other children of the same age or grade placement in the development of this skill?"

This book provides strategies for increasing your child's scores on both standardized norm-referenced and criterion-referenced tests.

The Major Standardized Tests

Many criterion-referenced tests currently in use are created locally or (at best) on a state level, and there are far too many of them to go into detail here about specific tests. However, children prepare for them in basically the same way they do for norm-referenced tests.

A very small pool of norm-referenced tests is used throughout the country, consisting primarily of the Big Five:

- California Achievement Tests (CTB/McGraw-Hill)
- Iowa Tests of Basic Skills (Riverside)
- Metropolitan Achievement Test (Harcourt-Brace & Company)
- Stanford Achievement Test (Psychological Corporation)
- TerraNova [formerly Comprehensive Test of Basic Skills] (McGraw-Hill)

These tests use various terms for the academic skills areas they assess, but they generally test several types of reading, language, and mathematics skills, along with social studies and science. They may include additional assessments, such as of study and reference skills.

How States Use Standardized Tests

Despite widespread belief and practice to the contrary, group standardized tests are designed to assess and compare the achievement of groups. They are *not* designed to provide detailed diagnostic assessments of individual students. (For detailed individual assessments, children should be given individual diagnostic tests by properly qualified professionals, including trained guidance counselors, speech and language therapists, and school psychologists.) Here are examples of the types of questions group standardized tests are designed to answer:

- How did the reading achievement of students at Valley Elementary School this year compare with their reading achievement last year?

- How did math scores at Wonderland Middle School compare with those of students at Parkside Middle School this year?

- As a group, how did Hilltop High School students compare with the national averages in the achievement areas tested?

- How did the district's first graders' math scores compare with the district's fifth graders' math scores?

The fact that these tests are designed primarily to test and compare groups doesn't mean that test data on individual students isn't useful. It does mean that when we use these tests to diagnose individual students, we are using them for a purpose for which they were not designed.

Think of group standardized tests as being similar to health fairs at the local mall. Rather than check into your local hospital and spend thousands of dollars on full, individual tests for a wide range of conditions, you can go from station to station and take part in different health screenings. Of course, one would never diagnose heart disease or cancer on the basis of the screening done at the mall. At most, suspicious results on the screening would suggest that you need to visit a doctor for a more complete examination.

In the same way, group standardized tests provide a way of screening the achievement of many students quickly. Although you shouldn't diagnose learning problems solely based on the results of these tests, the results can tell you that you should think about referring a child for a more definitive, individual assessment.

An individual student's group test data should be considered only a point of information. Teachers and school administrators may use standardized test results to support or question hypotheses they have made about students; but these scores must be used alongside other information, such as teacher comments, daily work, homework, class test grades, parent observations, medical needs, and social history.

Valid Uses of Standardized Test Scores

Here are examples of appropriate uses of test scores for individual students:

- Mr. Cone thinks that Samantha, a third grader, is struggling in math. He reviews her file and finds that her first- and second-grade standardized test math scores were very low. Her first- and second-grade teachers recall episodes in which Samantha cried because she couldn't understand certain math concepts, and mention that she was teased by other children, who called her "Dummy." Mr. Cone decides to refer Samantha to the school assistance team to determine whether she should be referred for individual testing for a learning disability related to math.

- The local college wants to set up a tutoring program for elementary school children who are struggling academically. In deciding which youngsters to nominate for the program, the teachers consider the students' averages in different subjects, the degree to which students seem to be struggling, parents' reports, and standardized test scores.

- For the second year in a row, Gene has performed poorly on the latest round of standardized tests. His teachers all agree that Gene seems to have some serious learning problems. They had hoped that Gene was immature for his class and that he would do better this year; but his dismal grades continue. Gene is referred to the school assistance team to determine whether he should be sent to the school psychologist for assessment of a possible learning handicap.

Inappropriate Use of Standardized Test Scores

Here are examples of how schools have sometimes used standardized test results inappropriately:

- Mr. Johnson groups his students into reading groups solely on the basis of their standardized test scores.

- Ms. Henry recommends that Susie be held back a year because she performed poorly on the standardized tests, despite strong grades on daily assignments, homework, and class tests.

- Gerald's teacher refers him for consideration in the district's gifted program, which accepts students using a combination of intelligence test scores, achievement test scores, and teacher recommendations. Gerald's intelligence test scores were very high. Unfortunately, he had a bad cold during the week of the standardized group achievement tests and was taking powerful antihistamines, which made him feel sleepy. As a result, he scored too low on the achievement tests to qualify.

The public has come to demand increasingly high levels of accountability for public schools. We demand that schools test so that we have hard data with which to hold the schools accountable. But too often, politicians and the public place more faith in the test results than is justified. Regardless of whether it's appropriate to do so and regardless of the reasons schools use standardized test results as they do, many schools base crucial programming and eligibility decisions on scores from group standardized tests. It's to your child's advantage, then, to perform as well as possible on these tests.

Two Basic Assumptions

The strategies we present in this book come from two basic assumptions:

1. Most students can raise their standardized test scores.

2. Parents can help their children become stronger in the skills the tests assess.

This book provides the information you need

to learn what skill areas the tests measure, what general skills your child is being taught in a particular grade, how to prepare your child to take the tests, and what to do with the results. In the appendices you will find information to help you decipher test interpretations; a listing of which states currently require what tests; and additional resources to help you help your child to do better in school and to prepare for the tests.

A Word about Coaching

This guide is *not* about coaching your child. When we use the term *coaching* in referring to standardized testing, we mean trying to give someone an unfair advantage, either by revealing beforehand what exact items will be on the test or by teaching "tricks" that will supposedly allow a student to take advantage of some detail in how the tests are constructed.

Some people try to coach students in shrewd test-taking strategies that take advantage of how the tests are supposedly constructed rather than strengthening the students' skills in the areas tested. Over the years, for example, many rumors have been floated about "secret formulas" that test companies use.

This type of coaching emphasizes ways to help students obtain scores they didn't earn—to get something for nothing. Stories have appeared in the press about teachers who have coached their students on specific questions, parents who have tried to obtain advance copies of tests, and students who have written down test questions after taking standardized tests and sold them to others. Because of the importance of test security, test companies and states aggressively prosecute those who attempt to violate test security—and they should do so.

How to Raise Test Scores

Factors that are unrelated to how strong students are but that might artificially lower test scores include anything that prevents students from making scores that accurately describe their actual abilities. Some of those factors are:

- giving the tests in uncomfortably cold or hot rooms;

- allowing outside noises to interfere with test taking; and

- reproducing test booklets in such small print or with such faint ink that students can't read the questions.

Such problems require administrative attention from both the test publishers, who must make sure that they obtain their norms for the tests under the same conditions students face when they take the tests; and school administrators, who must ensure that conditions under which their students take the tests are as close as possible to those specified by the test publishers.

Individual students also face problems that can artificially lower their test scores, and parents can do something about many of these problems. Stomach aches, headaches, sleep deprivation, colds and flu, and emotional upsets due to a recent tragedy are problems that might call for the student to take the tests during make-up sessions. Some students have physical conditions such as muscle-control problems, palsies, or difficulty paying attention that require work over many months or even years before students can obtain accurate test scores on standardized tests. And, of course, some students just don't take the testing seriously or may even intentionally perform poorly. Parents can help their children overcome many of these obstacles to obtaining accurate scores.

Finally, with this book parents are able to help their children raise their scores by:

- increasing their familiarity (and their comfort level) with the types of questions on standardized tests;

- drills and practice exercises to increase their skill in handling the kinds of questions they will meet; and

- providing lots of fun ways for parents to help their children work on the skill areas that will be tested.

Test Questions

The favorite type of question for standardized tests is the multiple-choice question. For example:

1. The first President of the United States was:

   A Abraham Lincoln

   B Martin Luther King, Jr.

   C George Washington

   D Thomas Jefferson

The main advantage of multiple-choice questions is that it is easy to score them quickly and accurately. They lend themselves to optical scanning test forms, on which students fill in bubbles or squares and the forms are scored by machine. Increasingly, companies are moving from paper-based testing to computer-based testing, using multiple-choice questions.

The main disadvantage of multiple-choice questions is that they restrict test items to those that can be put in that form. Many educators and civil rights advocates have noted that the multiple-choice format only reveals a superficial understanding of the subject. It's not possible with multiple-choice questions to test a student's ability to construct a detailed, logical argument on some issue or to explain a detailed process. Although some of the major tests are beginning to incorporate more subjectively scored items, such as short answer or essay questions, the vast majority of test items continue to be in multiple-choice format.

In the past, some people believed there were special formulas or tricks to help test-takers determine which multiple-choice answer was the correct one. There may have been some truth to *some* claims for past tests. Computer analyses of some past tests revealed certain biases in how tests were constructed. For example, the old advice to pick *D* when in doubt appears to have been valid for some past tests. However, test publishers have become so sophisticated in their ability to detect patterns of bias in the formulation of test questions and answers that they now guard against it aggressively.

In Chapter 1, we provide information about general test-taking considerations, with advice on how parents can help students overcome testing obstacles. The rest of the book provides information to help parents help their children strengthen skills in the tested areas.

Joseph Harris, Ph.D.

Test-Taking Basics

You can be sure that at some time during the 12 years that your children spend in school, they'll face a standardized testing situation. Some schools test every year, some test every other year—but at some point your child will be assessed. How well your child does on such a test can be related to many things—did he get plenty of rest the night before? Is he anxious in testing situations? Did he get confused when filling in the answer sheets and make a mechanical mistake?

That's why educators emphasize that a child's score on a standardized test shouldn't be used as the sole criterion of how that child is learning and developing. Instead, any test score should be evaluated as only one part of an educational picture that consists of the child's classroom performance and overall areas of strengths and weaknesses. Your child won't pass or fail a standardized test, but you can often see a general pattern of strengths and weaknesses.

What This Book Can Do

This book is not designed to help your child artificially inflate scores on a standardized test. Instead, it's meant to help you understand the typical kinds of skills taught in a second-grade class and what a typical second grader can be expected to know and to be able to do by the end of the second year. It also presents lots of fun activities that you can use at home to work with your child in particular skill areas that may be a bit weak.

Furthermore, this book is not meant to replace your child's teacher but rather to help you work with the teacher and the school as a team to help your child succeed.

Keep in mind, however, that endless drilling is not the best way to help your child improve. While most children want to do well and please their teachers and parents, they already spend about seven hours a day in school. Extracurricular activities, homework, and music and sports practice take up more time. To avoid overwhelming your child, try to use the activities in this book in reasonable doses to stimulate and support your child's work at school.

Most children entering the second grade are able to perform intricate fine-motor tasks such as writing, manipulating small items, and playing a musical instrument. You'll probably notice that your child has a much better sense of his body as he moves and is probably far less clumsy than even a year ago. Intellectually, you'll probably see that your second grader is becoming more logical as he begins to be able to see the world from another's perspective. Remember, however, that not all children learn things at the same rate. What may be typical for one second grader is certainly not the norm for another. You should use the information presented in this book in conjunction with school-work to help develop your child's essential skills in reading, grammar, and writing.

How to Use This Book

There are many different ways to use this book. Some children are quite strong in certain verbal areas, but they need a bit of help in other areas. Perhaps your child is a whiz at grammar but has some trouble with reading comprehension. Focus your attention on those skills that need some work, and spend more time on those areas.

You'll see in each chapter an introductory explanation of the material in the chapter, followed by a summary of what a typical child in second grade should be expected to know about that skill by the end of the year. This is followed in each chapter by an extensive section featuring interesting, fun, or unusual activities you can do with your child to reinforce the skills presented in the chapter. Most activities use only inexpensive items found around the home, and many are suitable for car trips, waiting rooms, and restaurants.

Next, you'll find an explanation of how typical standardized tests may assess that skill and what your child might expect to see on a typical test. We've included sample questions at the end of each section that are designed to help familiarize your child with the types of questions found on a typical standardized test. These questions do *not* measure your child's proficiency in any given content area; however, if you notice that your child is having trouble with a particular question, you can use that information to figure out what skills you need to focus on.

Basic Test-Taking Strategies

Sometimes children score lower on standardized tests than they do on other types of tests because they approach testing in an inefficient way. There are things you can do before the test—and that your child can do during the test—to make sure he does as well as he can.

Before the Test

Perhaps the most effective thing you can do to prepare your child for standardized tests is to be patient. Remember that no matter how much pressure you put on your children, they won't learn certain skills until they are physically, mentally, and emotionally ready to do so. You've got to walk a delicate line between challenging and pressuring your children. If you see your child isn't making progress or is getting frustrated, it may be time to lighten up.

Don't Change the Routine. Many experts offer mistaken advice about how to prepare children for a test, such as recommending that children go to bed early the night before or eat a high-protein breakfast on the morning of the test. It's a better idea not to alter your child's routine at all right before the test.

If your child isn't used to going to bed early, then sending him off at 7:30 p.m. the night before a test will only make it harder for him to get to sleep by the normal time. If he is used to eating an orange or a piece of toast for breakfast, forcing him to down a platter of fried eggs and bacon will only make him feel sleepy or uncomfortable.

Practice with Neatness. There is an incorrect way to fill in an answer sheet on a standardized test, and this type of error can really make a difference on the final results. It pays to give your child some practice on filling in answer sheets. Watch how neatly your child can fill in the bubbles, squares, and rectangles that follow. If he overlaps the lines, makes a lot of erasures, or presses the pencil too hard, try having him practice with pages of bubbles. You can easily create sheets of capital *O*'s, squares, and rectangles that your child can practice filling in. If he gets bored doing that, have him color in detailed pictures in coloring books, or complete connect-the-dots pages.

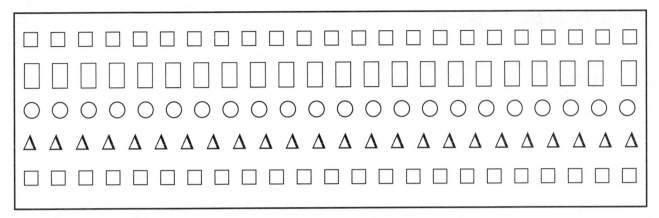

During the Test

There are some techniques that can be used to prepare for standardized testing that have been shown to make some degree of improvement in a score. Some of these techniques are given below. Discuss these strategies with your child from time to time.

Bringing Extra Pencils. You don't want your child spending valuable testing time jumping up to sharpen a pencil. Send along plenty of extra, well-sharpened pencils to standardized testing sessions.

Listening Carefully. You wouldn't believe how many errors kids make because they don't listen to instructions or they don't pay attention to demonstrations. Some children mark the wrong form, fill in the bubbles incorrectly, or skip to the wrong section. Others simply forget to put their names on the answer sheets. Many make a mark on the answer sheet without realizing that they are marking the wrong bubble.

Reading the Entire Question First. Some children get so excited about the test that they begin filling in bubbles before they finish reading the entire question. The last few words in a question sometimes give the most important clues to the correct answer.

Reading Carefully. In their desire to finish first, many children tend to select the first answer that seems right to them without thoroughly reading all the responses and choosing the very best answer. Make sure your child understands the importance of evaluating all the answers before choosing one.

Skipping Difficult Items; Returning to Them Later. Many children will sit and worry about a hard question, spending so much time on one problem that they never get to problems that they would be able to answer correctly if they had only left enough time. Explain to your child that he can always come back to a knotty question once he finishes the section.

Referring to Pictures for Clues. Tell your child not to overlook the pictures in the test booklets because they may reveal valuable clues as to the correct answers. Students can also find clues to correct answers by looking at descriptions, wording, and other information from the questions.

Using Key Words. Have your child look at the questions and try to figure out the parts that are important and those that aren't.

Eliminating Answer Choices. Just as in the wildly successful TV show *Who Wants to Be a Millionaire*, remind your child that it's a good idea to narrow down his choices among multiple-choice options by eliminating answers he knows can't possibly be true.

On to the Second Chapter

Now that you've learned a bit about the test-taking basics, it's time to turn your attention to the first of the reading skills—basic vocabulary.

CHAPTER 2

Vocabulary

To be a good reader and writer, a child must have a solid vocabulary. There's a lot you can do at home to boost the acquisition of words, both through the language you use and in fun games you play together.

The early years in school are a time of tremendous brain development, particularly in the areas that control how we speak to others and how we interpret what they say. This is the reason that you've seen such tremendous growth in vocabulary in kindergarten and first grade, which will continue in second.

Word Meanings

During second grade, your child will continue to develop both the words she recognizes when she hears (*receptive vocabulary*) and the words she uses when she speaks (*expressive vocabulary*).

Typically, receptive vocabulary is the first to develop because it is easier to understand language than it is to speak it. A child's receptive vocabulary is usually more fully developed than her expressive vocabulary, but as she gets older, the gap between the two lessens.

What Second Graders Should Know

By second grade you can expect your child to be a fluent conversationalist. Not only is she able to understand abstract concepts but you've probably begun to notice that she is starting to use abstract and complex concepts herself as well. As your child enters second grade, she will begin to develop abilities to describe thoughts and feelings precisely.

Most children enter second grade with a well-developed *picture vocabulary* (the ability to match words and pictures); through the year they will begin to make more complex deductions from those pictures. For example, an early first grader might describe a picture of a person leaping to his feet with a big smile on his face as a "person jumping," but a second grader might elaborate, saying that the person in the picture is excited or happy. Then she will correctly choose from among a series of pictures one that illustrates "winning a big prize in a contest." As your child ends second grade, she will continue to develop her abilities to describe thoughts and feelings.

What You and Your Child Can Do

Read and Read Some More! If you want your child to have an effective vocabulary, the best way to do that is to read to her. Read every day, and let her read aloud to you as well. Choose books on a wide range of subjects, and let your child choose books on her own as well. Be alert to her special hobbies or interests, and then provide books on those topics. You don't have to buy books—you can borrow as many books as your child can read from the local library. Encourage your child to read on her own, too, and let her see you read for pleasure.

Play Commercial Games. There are many commercial games that are good for boosting vocabulary. Games such as *Concentration* or *Password* are old favorites and can help boost vocabulary (although some may need to be simplified for a second grader's ability). *Scrabble Junior* is another great choice for second graders because it includes the use of pictures and beginning letters for early readers.

Take a Trip. You don't have to journey to Paris to find interesting places to take your second grader. Local outings to a museum, planetarium, or zoo will captivate her curiosity just as well. Whenever you go, encourage her to read the materials available. Help her to expand her interests because a curious child with lots of stimulation will almost automatically increase her vocabulary. If your child is interested in the weather, take her to the local TV station to watch a meteorologist at work. If she is interested in planes, visit your local airport. If she likes animals, join the local zoo society. The more she is exposed to and reads about the things that interest her, the better her vocabulary will be.

Talk to Your Child. Reading isn't the only way to boost vocabulary—conversation will also do the trick. In fact, the more language she hears, the better her vocabulary will be. It's a fact that children with a strong vocabulary tend to have parents with the same skills. But don't despair if your own vocabulary isn't the best. If the environment is stimulating, the child's vocabulary will improve.

Stump the Family. Each day, assign a member of your family to look up one new word and use it to try to stump the family at dinner. On her day, help your second grader look through a dictionary to find an unusual word. See if anyone can guess what the word means.

Build a Scaffold. One good way to boost your child's use of words is to build a verbal *scaffold*. That is, use a complex word and then define it in simpler terms right afterward. For example: Lauren's mother says: "Oh dear, the honey is *crystallizing*. It's forming little hard bits that won't melt." Children with the biggest vocabularies tend to have parents who automatically scaffold their sentences.

Define It. Of course, it's also fine for you to simply define words outright: "Your grandfather was *ambidextrous*. That means he could use his right hand just as well as he could use his left." Don't automatically use the simplest words to talk to your child, and certainly avoid baby talk. Speak to her as if she were older, and you might be surprised to see her vocabulary improve.

Play Hangman. This popular family game requires just a pencil and a scrap of paper—a great diversion during endless waits in the doctor's office or a restaurant. When it's your turn to give a word, don't use the simplest word you can think of. Use a more challenging choice and explain the word once the child has guessed all the letters.

Look It Up! You're never too old to learn new words. Let your second grader see you learn new words, too. When you come across a word you don't know, tell your child: "This article mentions the alimentary canal. You know, I've never really understood what part of the body that is. I'm going to look it up in the dictionary." Encourage your child to do the same thing. If she comes across an unfamiliar word, help her look it up in an age-appropriate dictionary.

Play Word Scramble. This ever-popular party game can be lots of fun for children to play, especially if you get several children together and offer a prize for the most words. To play word scramble, choose one larger word (such as *Thanksgiving*), and have children find as many smaller words as they can using the same letters. Set a time limit.

Use the Internet Wordfind. If your child doesn't enjoy using a dictionary, you may be able to reach her via cyberspace: Try one of the countless online dictionaries. While finding a word using the search key isn't teaching dictionary skills, it will enable you to capture her interest in learning new words. This is one good way to encourage computer-savvy reluctant readers.

What Tests May Ask

Standardized tests for second graders assess vocabulary development in several ways. Most often, these tests will present sentences with a word missing and ask children to fill in the blank with a correct word from a group of choices.

Practice Skill: Word Meanings

Directions: Choose the correct word to go in the blank in these sentences.

Example:

The kitten chased a ball of ____.

- (A) yarn
- (B) bone
- (C) hole
- (D) grass

Answer:

- (A) yarn

1 The teacher sent Jeff to the ____ to see the principal.
- (A) laundry
- (B) stone
- (C) office
- (D) eraser

2 Sharon looked everywhere, but she could not _____ the book.
- (A) hear
- (B) fear
- (C) find
- (D) lose

3 As it got dark, we heard a ____ howl.
- (A) car
- (B) worm
- (C) cow
- (D) wolf

4 Ellen was happy because her experiment was a _____.
- (A) failure
- (B) problem
- (C) success
- (D) good

(See page 133 for the answer key.)

Picture Vocabulary

Picture vocabulary refers to the words we recognize when we see illustrations of them. The ability to *name* objects in a picture is called *expressive picture vocabulary,* while the ability to *recognize* objects in a picture is called *receptive picture vocabulary.*

The ability to develop a good picture vocabulary is important in learning how to read. As you read to your child, she associates the pictures with the words she hears you read. Eventually, she develops the ability to read words without pictures. For example, when a picture book provides a picture of a dog with the word *dog* underneath, the child eventually associates the written word with the picture. Later, she learns to recognize that the printed word *dog* refers to a dog. Eventually, your child will have a larger receptive than expressive picture vocabulary.

What Second Graders Should Know

Given the popularity of picture books, by the time they are in second grade, most children are quite good at identifying pictures and figuring out what pictures mean. When they enter second grade, most children should be able to identify and interpret very simple abstract words from pictures. If given a choice of four pictures of a person with various facial expressions, a typical second grader should be able to select the person with a broad smile as "the happy one."

At this age, your child should be able to use pictures together with story patterns, context, and memory of some words to make sense of the printed vocabulary.

What You and Your Child Can Do

Picture Walk. Using a well-illustrated picture book, cover up the words and look through the book with your child, encouraging her to discuss what might be going on in the pictures. When you discuss the pictures, use as much of the actual language used in the text as possible—especially any words you think your child might not know.

Catalog Hunt. Second graders generally enjoy looking at the pretty pictures in catalogs. Try playing the *catalog scavenger hunt game*. Give your child a list of things to find in catalogs—either objects or people who have certain facial expressions or who are doing certain things. Tailor the items for the child to find to match the type of catalogs you have. For instance, you

might ask your child to find a picture of someone skiing if you have winter sports equipment catalogs. Print out the list of objects to be found on a sheet of stiff paper, and have your child cut and paste her treasures onto the sheet.

Photo Find. Another way to develop picture vocabulary utilizes the family photo album. Kids love looking at photos (especially pictures of themselves). As you turn the page, ask your second grader a series of questions: What are you doing in this picture? Then write a series of verbs on index cards (*riding, roller skating, swimming, diving, running, crying, laughing*). Then go back to the album, point to a photo and ask your child to select a card from a group of three or four that matches what she's doing in the photo.

Write a Story. Here's a good rainy-day activity if your child has a friend over to play. Have one child draw a series of pictures on several sheets of paper and staple them together (or cut out pictures from a magazine and paste them on paper). Have the other child write a story by printing a few words to go with each picture. She'll need to study the pictures carefully in order to come up with a likely tale. Then have the two children switch places.

What Tests May Ask

Standardized tests in second grade assess a child's ability to either name objects (expressive picture vocabulary) or recognize objects (receptive picture vocabulary) that the child sees in pictures.

A test question designed to gauge expressive picture vocabulary might ask the child to look at a picture and then choose the word that correctly describes what the subject of the picture is doing. To assess receptive picture vocabulary, the test could ask a child to read a word and then choose the one picture out of a group of pictures that correctly represents the word. This requires the child to retrieve from memory the label for what the picture shows. Or the test will present a picture and ask the child to choose its appropriate description from a group of possibilities.

Practice Skill: Picture Vocabulary

Directions: Look at each picture and choose the correct answer from the choices given below.

Example:

How does the girl in this picture feel?

Ⓐ sorry

Ⓑ proud

Ⓒ sad

Ⓓ brave

Answer:

Ⓑ proud

5 Which of the following pictures shows a child being kind?

Ⓐ

Ⓑ

Ⓒ

Ⓓ

6 Where is Jip the dog hiding?

(A) in the trees

(B) in the dog house

(C) in the bedroom

(D) in the attic

7 What is Sarah wearing?

(A) a swimsuit

(B) a dress

(C) shorts

(D) a raincoat

8 Which of these words tells what these dogs are doing?

(A) eating

(B) barking

(C) fighting

(D) playing

9 Which word tells what the child is doing?

(A) running

(B) eating

(C) fighting

(D) sleeping

10 Which picture shows the children sailing?

Ⓐ   Ⓑ

Ⓒ   Ⓓ

11 Which picture shows the boy fishing?

Ⓐ   Ⓑ

Ⓒ   Ⓓ

(See page 133 for the answer key.)

CHAPTER 3

Word Meanings in Context

When you pick up a best-seller, you probably don't think too much about the process of reading—you just read. And when you read individual sentences one by one, you may not realize that you don't focus on each word individually, as if it had no relationship to the words around it. Instead, you read each word within its context—as one complete whole.

Most adults take this for granted and don't really think about the process of reading, but when a child first learns to put words together, he doesn't look at a sentence as an unbroken whole. Instead, most children learn to read by reading individual words. Only later does the child begin to see the words in context of the entire sentence.

If your child is to become a good, confident reader, he must learn to understand not only what each word means but how it relates to the sentence as a whole. This ability to read in context will also help him decode unfamiliar words by figuring out their definition based on the rest of the sentence.

What Second Graders Should Know

When your child first began to read to you out loud, his words probably sounded a bit mechanical. This is because many children first learn to read by sounding out individual words. A beginning reader reads the words without any dramatic sense of understanding, with no changes in pace or inflection. Most likely, if a beginner reads the wrong word, he keeps on going even if it doesn't make a bit of sense. This is because early readers tend to read words individually, without an overall sense of the total meaning of the sentence.

By second grade, however, most children have begun to understand that the sentence as a whole should make sense. You'll begin to hear a cadence to his oral reading. If he comes to a word that doesn't make sense in the sentence, he will probably stop reading and either puzzle it out himself or ask for help.

At last, your child is beginning to understand the complete meaning of the combined elements in a sentence, and that skill will get better and better as your child gets older.

What You and Your Child Can Do

Read! Reading to your child—and having him read to you—will increase his vocabulary skills at an amazing rate. If he comes to a word he doesn't understand, have him stop and see if he can puzzle it out from the context of the sentence. Let him see how the sentence as a whole relates to other sentences.

Sentence Fun. While you're waiting to be served in a restaurant, try to work on context this way: Give your child a sentence with a word missing. See how many words he can think of that would fit in the blank and still make sense. Talk about which ones seem most logical.

What Tests May Ask

Most standardized tests will assess your child's ability to see and understand words in context. The tests will offer a sentence and ask the child to fill in the blank with the word that makes the most sense. This requires a child to understand which words do and don't fit into a sentence given a sentence's meaning, and it also requires your child to understand that a word may have more than one meaning.

Practice Skill: Word Meanings in Context

Directions: Read each sentence and choose the word that best fits in the blank.

Example:

It was time to go to sleep, so Sarah climbed into her _____.

Ⓐ sink

Ⓑ bed

Ⓒ bike

Ⓓ book

Answer:

Ⓑ bed

1 All but the _____ runners finished the race.

Ⓐ weakest

Ⓑ strongest

Ⓒ silliest

Ⓓ loudest

2 We were very _____ so we decided to nap.

Ⓐ rich

Ⓑ angry

Ⓒ hungry

Ⓓ tired

3 I was feeling _____ because my puppy was sick.

Ⓐ tired

Ⓑ sad

Ⓒ happy

Ⓓ silly

4 Kellen had to pay a fine at the library because his book was _____.

Ⓐ good

Ⓑ bad

Ⓒ late

Ⓓ green

5 Marcy wrapped her pony's foot in a _____ because it was sore.

    Ⓐ purse

    Ⓑ bandage

    Ⓒ ribbon

    Ⓓ book

6 Jim and Bill were _____ of the spooky Halloween noises.

    Ⓐ afraid

    Ⓑ wondering

    Ⓒ happy

    Ⓓ wild

7 Josh was afraid of the _____ tiger.

    Ⓐ smiling

    Ⓑ roaring

    Ⓒ mild

    Ⓓ meek

8 The _____ blew the shutters off the wall.

    Ⓐ moon

    Ⓑ sun

    Ⓒ wind

    Ⓓ stars

9 Becca loved to pet the puppy because he was so _____.

    Ⓐ sharp

    Ⓑ mean

    Ⓒ smart

    Ⓓ soft

10 After walking for 5 miles, Brittany was _____.

    Ⓐ tired

    Ⓑ ten

    Ⓒ laughing

    Ⓓ small

Directions: Read each sentence and choose the answer that means the same as the underlined word.

Example:

Sarah used a key to <u>unlock</u> the front door.

    Ⓐ slam

    Ⓑ close

    Ⓒ open

    Ⓓ park

Answer:

    Ⓒ open

11 Elizabeth <u>often</u> goes to the park.

    Ⓐ never

    Ⓑ seldom

    Ⓒ frequently

    Ⓓ sadly

12 It's <u>likely</u> that Mrs. Smith will give the class a test tomorrow.

    Ⓐ happily

    Ⓑ probable

    Ⓒ slow

    Ⓓ quick

13 Kristi was <u>satisfied</u> with her drawing of the cat.

   Ⓐ unhappy

   Ⓑ angry

   Ⓒ giggly

   Ⓓ pleased

---

14 The squirrels will <u>collect</u> nuts for the winter.

   Ⓐ throw away

   Ⓑ gather

   Ⓒ hit

   Ⓓ throw

---

15 The new student had <u>few</u> mistakes on her test.

   Ⓐ many

   Ⓑ lots

   Ⓒ limited

   Ⓓ none

---

16 The two girls <u>raced</u> around the track.

   Ⓐ walked

   Ⓑ skipped

   Ⓒ ran

   Ⓓ slept

Directions: Read the paragraph below. Find the words below the paragraph that best fit in each numbered blank.

Example:

Cassie and Kara had   __1__   at the slumber party. The two girls laughed all night with their __2__ .

1 Ⓐ doughnuts   **2** Ⓐ dogs

    Ⓑ fun   Ⓑ mothers

    Ⓒ dolphins   Ⓒ pancakes

    Ⓓ sad   Ⓓ friends

Answers:

  1 Ⓑ fun   **2** Ⓓ friends

Cassie, Lavon, and Wanda spent the day at the beach. They built castles, swam in the __17__ , and buried each other in the __18__ . For lunch they bought hot dogs and had a __19__ by the water. The __20__ felt warm on their skin. By the end of the long, busy day, they were very __21__ .

17 Ⓐ mud

     Ⓑ sea

     Ⓒ tub

     Ⓓ sink

18
- (A) sand
- (B) lava
- (C) stones
- (D) grass

19
- (A) test
- (B) cat
- (C) rain
- (D) picnic

20
- (A) chocolate
- (B) shells
- (C) sun
- (D) seaweed

21
- (A) poor
- (B) musical
- (C) tired
- (D) identical

(See page 133 for the answer key.)

CHAPTER 4

Synonyms, Antonyms, and Homonyms

A strong vocabulary is crucial to being a good writer and reader, and having a strong grasp of synonyms, antonyms, and homonyms will be a big help to your second grader. Because a basic understanding of "alike" and "different" is so vital to being a good reader, you can bet these concepts will be included on most standardized tests as well.

Synonyms are words that sound different but mean "the same as." *Big* and *huge* are typical examples of synonyms that second graders will be able to understand. *Antonyms* are words that have opposite meanings, such as *big* and *little*. These can be even more fun for second graders to practice. Although the terms *homophone* and *homonym* are often used interchangeably, technically they refer to quite different types of words. *Homonyms* (also called *multi-meaning words*) are spelled and sound the same, but they mean different things. For example, *bore* can be a noun (a person who isn't interesting) or a verb (the act of being uninteresting, or making a hole into something). Younger children can be quite inflexible with such words and insist that *air* means what you breathe and can't mean the same thing as *a song*. *Homophones* are words that sound the same but are spelled differently (such as *heir* and *air*).

Synonyms

What Second Graders Should Know

Most second graders can understand the fact that two different words can mean the same

thing, although most won't understand the term *synonym*. Most will be quite accurate at simple comparisons, such as *big* and *large*. Because your child is beginning to understand abstract and complex terms, she'll be able to identify some synonyms that refer to basic abstract words.

For example, your child will probably be able to tell you that *pretty* and *beautiful* mean the same thing. In contrast to a first grader, who insists that *sofa* and *couch* are different, your second grader will be much more flexible and will understand that these two words refer to the same object. This doesn't mean that your child is quite ready for one-way relationships, such as realizing that while all trout are fish, not all fish are trout.

What You and Your Child Can Do

Playing word games with synonyms can be lots of fun and simple to do at home. If your child has trouble remembering the difference between *synonym* and *antonym*, tell her that *synonym* and *same as* both begin with the same letter: *s*. *Antonym* and *anti* (against or opposite) both begin with *a*.

Top It! This game is great to play anytime, since you don't need any props. Try it during a long wait at a restaurant or the doctor's office. One player starts off with a simple sentence: "I'm cold." The next person tries to "top the phrase"— "I'm freezing!" The first person then counters: "I'm shivering!" The second person then says:

"I'm frostbitten!" The game continues until no one can think of any more synonyms for the one word. Then you can begin all over again with new words.

Fill in the Blank. Here's another great restaurant game. The first person comes up with a word, and then the second person must find a synonym, and so on around the table:

MOM: Big.

SALLY: Tall.

BOB: Gigantic.

SUE: Huge.

Play continues until no more synonyms can be found.

Concentration. This game takes a little preparation by Mom or Dad up front, but once the cards are made, you can play the game over and over.

1. Take a stack of 10 index cards, and print a pair of synonyms on each card, such as *big* and *large*.

2. Cut each card in two to separate the synonyms.

3. Mix them up and turn them face down.

4. One by one, each player turns over two cards. If the two cards are a synonym, the player gets to keep the cards. If they aren't, the cards are turned over face down again, and play continues to the next player.

5. At the end of the game, the player with the most cards wins.

Guessing Games. These games make good car entertainment because they don't require pencil or paper. Start off this way:

YOU: I'm thinking of a word whose synonym means "gorgeous."

CHILD: Beautiful!

YOU: No, that's not it.

CHILD: Lovely!

YOU: Good guess, but not the one I'm thinking of.

CHILD: Pretty!

YOU: That's it!

Rephrasing Games. Children don't learn just from reading books; they learn just as much from talking to you on an everyday basis. When you're chatting, try rephrasing to expand your child's vocabulary:

CHILD: What a pretty kitten!

YOU: Yes, that kitten is really *beautiful*, isn't he! That's a *gorgeous* color.

What Tests May Ask

Standardized tests for second graders will assess a child's understanding of similarities in several ways. Some questions may ask youngsters to choose a synonym for an underlined word in a sentence from among a group of possibilities, or the test may present groups of two words and ask your child to choose the pair of words that mean the same thing. Then your child may be asked to choose a pair of words from a list that do *not* mean the same thing.

All these variations on the synonym theme are trying to make sure your child understands that it's possible for two different words to carry the same meaning.

Practice Skill: Synonyms

Directions: Look at the underlined word in each sentence. Which word is a *synonym* (a word that means the same thing) for the underlined word?

Example:

I'm <u>glad</u> the storm is over.

- Ⓐ happy
- Ⓑ afraid
- Ⓒ sorry
- Ⓓ mad

Answer:

- Ⓐ happy

---

1 Sam looked at the book and didn't know where to <u>begin</u>.

- Ⓐ smile
- Ⓑ start
- Ⓒ stop
- Ⓓ run

---

2 Chinda knew she would have to <u>clean</u> the plate.

- Ⓐ dry
- Ⓑ howl
- Ⓒ wash
- Ⓓ stack

---

3 The <u>small</u> ant worked very hard.

- Ⓐ busy
- Ⓑ silly
- Ⓒ tiny
- Ⓓ huge

---

4 The pup curled up to <u>rest</u> on the rug.

- Ⓐ sleep
- Ⓑ bark
- Ⓒ run
- Ⓓ growl

Directions: Choose the pair of words below that mean the same thing.

Example:

- Ⓐ listen   laugh
- Ⓑ close   near
- Ⓒ rabbit   horse
- Ⓓ hurry   stop

Answer:

- Ⓑ close   near

5
- Ⓐ black   white
- Ⓑ listen   talk
- Ⓒ slip   slide
- Ⓓ fast   slow

6
- Ⓐ carrot   lettuce
- Ⓑ sang   sat
- Ⓒ leaped   ate
- Ⓓ quick   fast

---

7 Ⓐ cry   sob

    Ⓑ jump   fall

    Ⓒ eat   drink

    Ⓓ round   square

(See page 133 for the answer key.)

Antonyms

Antonyms are words that mean the opposite, and it's clear that opposites attract second graders. Point out to your child that authors often use certain words (such as *but* or *however* to signal that an opposite is being used). For example, "I thought she was going to wear a *long* dress, but that one was *short.*"

What Second Graders Should Know

Last year, your first grader probably lacked a certain depth of understanding when it came to opposites; her comprehension of differences among words was probably limited to concrete comparisons that relied on tangible properties, such as "up" versus "down."

However, by mid to late second grade your child should start to have a better grasp of the complexity and abstraction of comparisons. For example, second graders will learn to recognize that *cheap* means the opposite of *expensive*. In most schools, the term *antonym* isn't introduced until third or fourth grade, but most second graders are quite talented at choosing opposites no matter what they're called.

What You and Your Child Can Do

Antonym Matching Game. In this game, your child will be matching up opposites instead of synonyms in a twist on the old "concentration" game.

1. Gather a stack of 10 index cards and write antonyms, one on each half of each index card.

2. Cut apart the two words on each index card.

3. Turn them face down and arrange them in five lines, two cards to a line.

4. Have the first child turn over two cards. If they are antonyms, she gets to keep the cards. If not, the cards are turned back face down and the next player begins.

Opposite Day. Speak in opposites for this word game: "I was up really late last night. Now I'm really awake" instead of "Now I'm really tired." Or "That hamburger really made me hungry" instead of "That hamburger really filled me up."

Antonym Bingo. Here's a fun twist on an old favorite. Make your own antonym bingo cards using antonym pairs appropriate for a second grader. Here are some to get you started: *add/subtract, after/before, bad/good, big/little, buy/sell, cold/warm, dark/light, mad/happy, early/late, love/hate, more/less, open/close, back/front, rich/poor, sick/well, slow/fast, soft/hard, tall/short,* and *young/old.*

Next, make the game boards:

1. Cut game boards from oaktag or thick paper, and divide the boards into 20 equal squares.

2. Print the first words of the antonym pairs on the game boards (make each board different).

3. Print the matching word of each antonym pair on index cards.

4. Each player chooses a game board and 10 chips.

5. The leader reads a word from the deck of index cards. The players look on their game boards for the matching antonyms. If they find a match, they cover the word with a chip.

6. The first player to cover a row horizontally, diagonally, or vertically calls out "Antonym bingo!"

New Word. The next time your child asks you the meaning of a new word, include the antonym as well as the definition or synonym:

CHILD: What does *sorrow* mean?

YOU: *Sorrow* means the same as *sadness*. The opposite of *sorrow* is *happiness*.

Riddle a Riddle. While driving on errands or on a family trip, try making up a riddle for your child to solve, utilizing antonyms: "I mean the opposite of *little* and I rhyme with *pig*." or "I mean the opposite of *soft* and I rhyme with *lard*." In this game, not only is your child learning about antonyms but she's also learning how to analyze words.

What Tests May Ask

Standardized tests for second graders will assess a child's understanding of opposites in much the way that synonyms are measured. Some questions may ask youngsters to choose an antonym for an underlined word in a sentence from among a group of possibilities. Tests may present groups of two words and ask your child to choose the pair of words that mean the opposite. Then your child may be asked to choose a pair of words from a list that **do** mean the same thing. All these variations on the antonym theme are trying to make sure your child's vocabulary is growing to the point where she can choose opposite words.

Practice Skill: Antonyms

Directions: Look at the sentences and pick the word that means the *opposite* of the word that is underlined.

Example:

Josh's experiment was a <u>success.</u>

(A) achievement
(B) happy
(C) experiment
(D) failure

Answer:

(D) failure

---

8 Amy <u>forgot</u> Elena's telephone number.

(A) missed
(B) learned
(C) telephone
(D) remembered

---

9 Josh was <u>sad</u> that his team lost the game.

(A) angry
(B) happy
(C) jealous
(D) surprised

---

10 Sally was too <u>short</u> to reach the ball.

(A) green
(B) tiny
(C) tall
(D) inside

---

11 Mother <u>opened</u> the door.

   Ⓐ closed

   Ⓑ painted

   Ⓒ brought

   Ⓓ dried

Directions: Choose the pair of words that are opposite in meaning.

Example:

   Ⓐ run   race

   Ⓑ angry   mad

   Ⓒ green   white

   Ⓓ push   pull

Answer:

   Ⓓ push   pull

---

12 Ⓐ ears   face

     Ⓑ string spring

     Ⓒ inside outside

     Ⓓ place   house

---

13 Ⓐ circle round

     Ⓑ insect bug

     Ⓒ walk   run

     Ⓓ house home

---

14 Ⓐ hard   soft

     Ⓑ fast   quick

     Ⓒ small   tiny

     Ⓓ still   quiet

(See page 133 for the answer key.)

Homonyms and Homophones

As discussed earlier in the chapter, the terms *homophone* and *homonym* are often used interchangeably, but technically they refer to quite different types of words. Remember that *homonyms* are spelled and sound the same, but they mean different things. For example, *brush* can be a noun (what you use on your hair) or a verb ("I'm going to brush my hair"). *Homophones* are words that sound the same but are spelled differently (such as *pear* and *pair).*

What Second Graders Should Know

By second grade, children have encountered such a wide variety of uses of different words that they are getting more flexible. Most are willing to accept that a word can have multiple meanings. But because children this age are still developing this skill, it's not at all unusual for some to continue to be moderately frustrated when confronted with these multi-meaning words.

What You and Your Child Can Do

Homonym Lists. Explain to the players that homonyms are two words that are spelled and sound alike but have different meanings. Set a timer and see how many homonyms you can come up with in three minutes. Gradually increase time as players get more experienced. For a less intimidating experience, have your child play with a partner. Play until no one can think of any more.

Detective. Send your child on a word hunt, looking for items that have a second meaning—for example, the *batter* in your mixing bowl and a *batter* in a baseball game. Have your child make a list of these words and keep it on the fridge. See how long the list can get.

Magazine Find. Give your child some old catalogs or magazines and have her cut out pictures of objects that have two or more meanings. Let her paste them into a notebook and see how many she can collect.

Homophone Matching Game. Take a set of index cards, and write pairs of homophones. Turn the index cards face down, and have your child turn over two at a time, trying to find a match.

Amelia Bedelia. This classic children's book series is filled with wonderful homophones that kids just love. Read this book together with your child. Then have your child write a paragraph with a main character like Amelia Bedelia, using at least five homophones. After writing the paragraph, have the child draw a picture of the homophone pair.

What Tests May Ask

Standardized tests for second grade may include some questions on multi-meaning words. It will be very important that your child read these questions carefully because it's easy to get confused about what the directions are asking for. Typically, the test will provide a sentence with an underlined word, and ask your child to select the homonym or homophone from a list of choices.

Practice Skill: Homonyms and Homophones

Directions: Read the following sentences and choose the correct word to fill in the blank.

Example:

_____ will be a party at noon.

Ⓐ They're

Ⓑ Their

Ⓒ There

Ⓓ Noon

Answer:

Ⓒ There

---

15 Her mother taught her how to _____ her own clothing.

Ⓐ so

Ⓑ sow

Ⓒ sew

Ⓓ sol

---

16 The kitten crawled into her _____. Later she began to ____ up some milk.

Ⓐ drink

Ⓑ sit

Ⓒ lip

Ⓓ lap

---

17 Sarah went to open a ___ of cat food. I don't think she ___ do it.

Ⓐ cat

Ⓑ can

Ⓒ could

Ⓓ will

(See page 133 for the answer key.)

CHAPTER 5

Word Sounds

Word sounds continue to be an important part of the second-grade curriculum in most schools. The study of word sounds in second grade includes learning how to identify both beginning and ending consonant sounds, consonant blends and digraphs, and vowel sounds.

Consonant Sounds

The study of consonant sounds includes both beginning and ending consonant sounds (such as the S in *Sun* or the ending S in *catS*). A consonant blend is the sound created when two consonants together are both heard at either the beginning or ending of a word:

GRoup   or   STrike

deSK   or   teST

Consonant digraphs are those double consonants that blend together into one sound: WH, CH, SH, and TH.

What Second Graders Should Know

As your child enters second grade, he may at first be confused about initial consonant sounds. However, by middle to late second grade, you'll see that he begins to recognize single and multiple consonant sounds at the beginning of words.

Word endings are another matter. In first grade, most children were confused by many word ending sounds, in part because of confusion over the word *ending*. But as their intellectual development continues, by second grade

most children will suddenly develop very acute abilities to identify ending word sounds. Most, for example, will be quite accurate at detecting single-consonant endings (such as *saT*) and both beginning and ending consonant blends (like *soNG*). Likewise, second graders should be skilled at picking out consonant digraphs such as CH or WH.

What You and Your Child Can Do

Felt Board. A felt board can help a lot to practice consonant beginnings and endings. You can make one by gluing one large piece of felt onto a large square of stiff cardboard, or tacking felt onto a bulletin board. Then buy, or cut out, letters of felt in a contrasting color, together with pictures of simple objects, such as a cat, a dog, and a cow. Apply a series of the objects to the felt board, and then ask your child to apply the corresponding beginning or ending sound. Time him if you want for extra fun.

Alternatively, apply a series of consonants onto the board, and ask your child to find an object with the corresponding beginning or ending sound.

Dishy Digraphs. Here's an activity that's sure to please any second grader. Since one of the most common digraphs (CH) is the beginning for the word *chocolate,* try this one out on make-your-own-sundae night at your house. As you sit around the table trying out toppings, point out how many digraphs are contained in these delicious desserts. Challenge your child to see how many he can come up with: Does he like CHocolate, with WHipped cream, and a CHerry? How about CHopped walnuts? You'll be amazed at how many you can come up with.

Guessing Game. During a long car ride or restaurant wait, play the "I'm thinking of" game: "I'm thinking of a word that starts with the hard K sound" (*key*).

Word Sound Card Game. Get a pack of multi-colored index cards. With a marker, print two cards each of these common consonants: B, C, D, G, K, L, M, P, R, S, and T (all of the same color). Now make another set using different color index cards printing these common letter patterns:

AT, AN, AT, EN, ET, IN, ING,

OP, OT, UG, UST, IT

Put the consonant cards face down in the middle of the table. Next, deal five of the letter pattern cards to each player. Each player draws a consonant card from the pile on the table and tries to make a word using any of the letter pattern cards in his hand (such as R + OT or T + AN). Any matches are laid down on the table in front of the player, who says the word out loud. When the player makes a word, his turn continues, and he can draw another consonant from the pile. If he can make still another match, he lays that one down. He may continue to play until he can't make a match. If he can't match the consonant with any word pattern in his hand, he puts the consonant card back on the bottom of the deck, and play continues to his left.

Computer Games. To help your child sound out more than 350 words, try *Kid Phonics 2* (Davidson & Associates), designed for children aged 6 through 9.

Also a good bet: *Schoolhouse Rock* (Creative Wonders), which offers games teaching reading and language arts, and *Word Munchers Deluxe*

(MECC/Softkey) that provides more than 6000 words in five difficulty levels.

Consonant Concentration. In this game, you can focus on *cluster consonants*—those consonants that appear in triplicate (such as SCReam or SPLash). Make a list of as many words with cluster consonants as you can. When you've got an even number (12 is good), write them down twice on individual index cards. Cut each index card in half so that you have 24 cards with one word each. Now turn them face down, and play as you would a regular game of concentration: Each player turns over two cards. If they match, the player "wins" those cards and takes another turn. The player with the most cards at the end of the game wins.

What Tests May Ask

Standardized tests will include questions on both beginning and ending consonant sounds. Questions may attempt to distract the child with similar sounds, which might have tripped up first graders. However, by late second grade (when most standardized tests are given), most students should be skilled at identifying ending sounds and able to choose the correct answer from similar-sounding choices.

Practice Skill: Beginning Word Sounds

Directions: Which pair of words *begins* with the same sound?

Example:

Ⓐ ball   put

Ⓑ city   cow

Ⓒ car   kind

Ⓓ get   gypsy

Answer:

   ⓒ car   kind

1 Ⓐ child   cat
   Ⓑ think   toad
   ⓒ cap   king
   Ⓓ jig   goat

2 Ⓐ jewel   jar
   Ⓑ choose cool
   ⓒ glove   giant
   Ⓓ cage   church

3 Ⓐ cookie   cent
   Ⓑ circus   card
   ⓒ shoot   shine
   Ⓓ chug   candy

4 Choose the word that has the same <u>beginning</u> sound as in <u>bread</u>.
   Ⓐ place
   Ⓑ bridge
   ⓒ acre
   Ⓓ print

5 Choose the word with the same <u>beginning</u> sound as in <u>cool</u>.
   Ⓐ kitchen
   Ⓑ school
   ⓒ pine
   Ⓓ go

Directions: Choose the letter that makes the beginning sound for each picture below.

Example:

   Ⓐ P
   Ⓑ R
   ⓒ K
   Ⓓ M

Answer:

   Ⓑ R

6 Ⓐ R
   Ⓑ T
   ⓒ Q
   Ⓓ L

Practice Skill: Ending Word Sounds

Directions: Choose the word with the same ending sound.

Example:

Which of these words has the same <u>ending</u> sound as the word <u>heart</u>?

Ⓐ deal

Ⓑ road

Ⓒ seat

Ⓓ meal

Answer:

Ⓒ seat

7 Ⓐ L

Ⓑ R

Ⓒ S

Ⓓ W

8 Ⓐ R

Ⓑ S

Ⓒ D

Ⓓ T

10 Which of these words has the same <u>ending</u> sound as the word <u>porch</u>?

Ⓐ church

Ⓑ hiss

Ⓒ fish

Ⓓ beat

11 Which of these words has the same <u>ending</u> sound as the word <u>beach</u>?

Ⓐ fit

Ⓑ peas

Ⓒ hit

Ⓓ hitch

9 Ⓐ K

Ⓑ R

Ⓒ H

Ⓓ Y

(See page 133 for the answer key.)

12 Which of these words has the same <u>ending</u> sound as the word <u>bass</u>?

Ⓐ faith

Ⓑ bat

Ⓒ birch

Ⓓ cats

13 Which of these words has the same <u>ending</u> sound as the word <u>seat</u>?

Ⓐ start

Ⓑ near

Ⓒ tease

Ⓓ church

Directions: Choose the letter that makes the ending sound for each picture below.

Example:

Ⓐ S

Ⓑ R

Ⓒ E

Ⓓ K

Answer:

Ⓓ K

14

Ⓐ Q

Ⓑ C

Ⓒ L

Ⓓ T

15

Ⓐ Q

Ⓑ C

Ⓒ N

Ⓓ K

16

Ⓐ K

Ⓑ L

Ⓒ M

Ⓓ S

(See page 133 for answer key.)

Consonant Blends

When two or more consonants are beside each other, the consonant sounds "blend" together, although each sound is heard. For example, in the word *black* you hear the B, but you also hear the L—because the two consonants are next to each other.

What Second Graders Should Know

By the end of second grade, your child will have learned the beginning concept of the consonant blend; that two consonants together "blend," but that each sound is heard separately. Your child should be able to identify these blends in speaking and reading.

What You and Your Child Can Do

Tongue Twisters. Here's a fun way to practice consonant blends. Have your child make up a tongue twister using consonant blends of all one kind. For example, for the consonant blend BL, you could try: Bleating blind blueberries blow blaringly in the blue sky. Or the GR blend: Great gray-green grilled grapes grope into the gruel.

Felt Board. Many of the same games children played to learn consonants can also be used for consonant blends. Using that same felt board, buy (or cut out) letter blends in a contrasting color. Apply a series of the objects to the felt board and then ask your child to apply the corresponding blending sound. Time him for extra fun.

Alternatively, apply a series of blend letters onto the board, and ask your child to find an object with the same beginning or ending sound.

Guessing Game. Another consonant game that can be adapted to teaching blends is the guessing game described earlier: "I'm thinking of a word that starts with the blend ST (*stone*)."

Sentence Salad. In this activity, you can help teach your child consonant blends. First, sit down with your child and together think up consonant blends for nouns, verbs, and adjectives. Take a stack of index cards, and print one word on each card. Place the cards face down in three piles (nouns, verbs, and adjectives). Now have your child choose one card from each pile and create a sentence using these words.

Timed End Blends. Players gather around a stack of index cards that have been marked with ending consonant blends, such as SK, NT, ST, MP, and FT. Set a timer for one or two minutes (or more, depending on the players' ages), and then everyone writes down as many words that end in the consonant blend as they can. The winner is the player with the most words.

What Tests May Ask

Standardized tests will include questions on consonant blends, including some questions that may attempt to distract a child with similar sounds. Late second graders should be skilled at identifying consonant blends and able to choose the correct answer from similar-sounding choices

Practice Skill: Consonant Blends

Directions: Choose the letters that make the beginning sound for each word below.

Example:

tree

Ⓐ T

Ⓑ TR

Ⓒ TH

Ⓓ TCH

Answer:

Ⓑ TR

17 sheep

  (A) CH

  (B) S

  (C) SP

  (D) SH

18 sleep

  (A) S

  (B) SP

  (C) ST

  (D) SL

19 when

  (A) WH

  (B) W

  (C) WE

  (D) H

20 growl

  (A) G

  (B) R

  (C) GE

  (D) GR

Directions: Choose the letters that make the ending sound for each word below.

Example:

lamp

  (A) MP

  (B) NP

  (C) P

  (D) ST

Answer:

  (A) MP

21 fist

  (A) T

  (B) SP

  (C) ST

  (D) SL

22 disk

  (A) CH

  (B) CK

  (C) K

  (D) SK

23 fast

  (A) ST

  (B) S

  (C) T

  (D) SH

(See page 133 for the answer key.)

Vowel Sounds

English is a language with complicated and sometimes unpredictable rules for vowel sounds that can stump many early readers. But the parts of the brain that govern sophisticated vowel sounds undergoes tremendous development between the ages of 6 and 8, and by second grade the brain structures are in place to allow most children to easily handle beginning lessons in vowels.

What Second Graders Should Know

While early readers may not see much point in studying vowels, by late second grade most children will know what vowels are and will be able to identify basic vowel sounds such as "the vowels that say their name" (as in the A sound in *rate*). They also will be able to identify different sounds made by the same vowels (such as the O sound in *hop* and *both*) and sounds made by vowel combinations such as in *boat* and *tear*.

What You and Your Child Can Do

Hangman. That popular old favorite is good for building a wide variety of verbal skills, including helping children to understand and learn vowels. Explain to your child that all words must have vowels, and a good way to begin guessing the letters for a word in hangman is to begin with each vowel: A, E, I, O, and U. As your child becomes more sophisticated with word play, he will see that in English, certain vowels are likely to occur in combination, or in certain locations in a word (that is, most words will have a vowel as the second or third letter).

Guess the Word. In this game, you try to get your child to guess the vowel sound:

PARENT: I'm thinking of a three-letter word that means an animal, and it has the vowel A that says its name.

CHILD: Cat!

What Tests May Ask

You can bet that standardized tests will include questions on vowel sounds, and they may include distracting questions with similar sounds. By late second grade, most students should be skilled at identifying vowel sounds,

and they will be able to confidently pick the correct answer from similar-sounding choices.

Practice Skill: Vowel Sounds

Directions: Match the word with the same vowel sound as the underlined word in each question.

Example:

Which word has the same *vowel* sound as in <u>toad</u>?

Ⓐ booth

Ⓑ rode

Ⓒ tap

Ⓓ hop

Answer:

Ⓑ rode

_____

24 What word has the same *vowel* sound as in <u>hat</u>?

Ⓐ hop

Ⓑ had

Ⓒ head

Ⓓ hip

_____

25 What word has the same *vowel* sound as in <u>light</u>?

Ⓐ star

Ⓑ bite

Ⓒ coat

Ⓓ fat

_____

26 What word has the same *vowel* sound as in <u>book</u>?

Ⓐ brought

Ⓑ school

Ⓒ took

Ⓓ bake

27 What word has the same *vowel* sound as in <u>team</u>?

Ⓐ taught

Ⓑ tight

Ⓒ mat

Ⓓ feet

(See page 133 for the answer key.)

CHAPTER 6

Word Recognition

In second grade, certain brain structures begin to develop that enable a child to understand many more spoken and written words. As a result, most parents of second graders notice an explosion in the number of new words children begin to understand, as the children's ability to read and understand takes off. At the same time, there is a monumental increase in the number of sight words they recognize when they see them in writing. This is the age when most children really begin to read well independently, and as they do this, they come across more and more new words.

Word Recognition

What Second Graders Should Know

Well-read second graders will be especially strong at recognizing new words. Many schools today are encouraging earlier familiarization with dictionaries, which also encourages word recognition skills. The typical words that second graders learn will be simple one- and two-syllable words that either follow standard phonetic rules or are very common.

What You and Your Child Can Do

Play 20 Questions. In this simple game, one person chooses a common word (such as *horse* or *boat*), and then she must describe it to the other players. For example, if the player chooses *dog*:

CHILD: It's an animal with four feet.

PLAYER: Horse!

CHILD: No. It's an animal with four feet that is shorter.

PLAYER: "Goat"

CHILD: No, it's an animal with four feet that are not hooves that is shorter.

PLAYER: Cat!

CHILD: No, It's an animal with four feet that are not hooves, that's shorter, and that barks.

PLAYER: Dog!

Read. As always, the best way to improve your child's ability to recognize new words is to read to her and have her read to you. If she comes to a word she's not sure about, don't immediately leap in and help. See if she can puzzle it out on her own. You both may be surprised at how well this works!

Make a Card. Another way to boost word recognition is to practice using words. Having your child make her own cards is a fun way to do just that. She can make greetings for any of the holidays. Encourage her to compose her own poem. After trying it out on scratch paper, let her create the final card on good thick paper. If she wants help with words, spelling, or usage, go ahead and help. Let her decorate it with drawings or pictures cut from magazines.

What Tests May Ask

Standardized tests assess word recognition in a fairly straightforward way. Most tests will present a definition and ask your child to select the correct answer, or they will present a word and ask the child to find the correct definition.

Practice Skill: Word Recognition

Directions: Choose the word that best fits the definition given in each of the following questions.

Example:

Which of these words means something we use to tell time?

Ⓐ watch

Ⓑ stick

Ⓒ fire

Ⓓ match

Answer:

Ⓐ watch

1 Which of these words means to attach two pieces of material?

Ⓐ ride

Ⓑ sew

Ⓒ bake

Ⓓ iron

2 Which of these words means to move snow?

Ⓐ drive

Ⓑ shovel

Ⓒ skate

Ⓓ jump

3 Which of these words means to take the wrinkles out of clothes?

Ⓐ wash

Ⓑ dry

Ⓒ iron

Ⓓ clean

4 Which of these words means to try to catch a trout?

Ⓐ swim

Ⓑ fly

Ⓒ fish

Ⓓ boat

5 Which of these words means to catch an animal?

Ⓐ fight

Ⓑ share

Ⓒ teach

Ⓓ trap

Directions: Choose the definition that goes with each word.

Example:

Which of the definitions goes with the word pay?

Ⓐ to give money for something

Ⓑ to have fun with a board game

Ⓒ to take with asking

Ⓓ to make a statue of a person

Answer:

Ⓐ to give money for something

6 Which of the definitions goes with the word <u>cook</u>?

(A) clean the stove

(B) take a picture of someone

(C) put some food into the refrigerator

(D) fry two eggs in a pan

7 Which of the definitions goes with the word <u>car</u>?

(A) something that you can sleep in

(B) something you can put food into

(C) object that you drive

(D) underground thing that you can explore

8 Which of the definitions goes with the word <u>pencil</u>?

(A) something you use to hold cattle

(B) something you use to draw

(C) something you use to hold two pieces of cloth together

(D) something you use to eat

(See page 133 for the answer key.)

Compound Words

Compound words are created by combining two smaller words, such as *stair* and *case* to make *staircase*.

What Second Graders Should Know

By second grade, most children will have realized that many words in English have been modified and combined to use in a new way. As our language evolves, we often combine two or more words to make new words, sometimes with meanings that have nothing to do with the original words. These are called *compound words,* and examples are *scarecrow, steamboat,* and *spaceship*.

What You and Your Child Can Do

Compound Jumble. Print a number of nouns on index cards. Have your child form as many compound words from these cards as possible.

Compounding Compounds. Encourage your second grader to keep a notebook filled with favorite compound words. See how many she can accumulate.

Crazy Compounds. Using the index cards you made in Compound Jumble, have your child try to form deliberately silly compounds and make up crazy definitions for them. For example: "Foghat. A hat to wear in the fog."

Compound Wordfind. Give your child a magazine or newspaper and a highlighter. Set the stopwatch for two minutes and have her highlight as many compound words as she can find.

Sticky Note Scavenger Hunt. Write down a list of compound words. Start with 10. Write the first part of the compound word on a sticky note, and tape it somewhere in the house with a blank sticky note beside it. Send your child off to find all 10 sticky notes; when your child finds one, have her finish the compound word. (For example, *sun*—could be *sunshine* or *sunbeam* or *suntan*.) Gather up the notes and read them together. For an extra challenge, try a backward compound hunt: write the second half of a compound word, and ask your child to come up with the beginning. (So —*ball* might be *baseball* or *football* or *softball*.)

What Tests May Ask

In second grade, standardized tests will include some questions about compound words by asking students to choose the compound word from a group of words.

Practice Skill: Compound Words

Directions: Choose the word that is made up of two words in the following questions.

Example:

  Ⓐ baseball

  Ⓑ scare

  © falcon

  Ⓓ tighten

Answer:

  Ⓐ baseball

---

9 Ⓐ rainbow

   Ⓑ street

   © foolish

   Ⓓ running

---

10 Ⓐ hunted

    Ⓑ skated

    © steamboat

    Ⓓ seen

---

11 Ⓐ boat

    Ⓑ jumping

    © hiding

    Ⓓ sunbeam

---

12 Ⓐ dog

    Ⓑ cat

    © Thanksgiving

    Ⓓ eat

(See page 133 for the answer key.)

Contractions

When children learn English, without thinking about it they learn to speak in contractions almost automatically. They rarely say "I will go to the store now." Instead, they shorten it to "I'll go to the store now." It's not until much later—usually first grade—that children are taught what those contractions we all use really mean. Even then, the instruction emphasizes simple, basic combinations such as *have + not = haven't*.

What Second Graders Should Know

In contrast to the basic understanding most first graders have of simple contractions, most second graders can use basic contractions easily. They are also able to identify the words that were combined to form the contractions.

What You and Your Child Can Do

Flash Cards. Using index cards, make a series of flash cards for contractions:

Will not

Cannot

It is

Is not

Do not

I will

Would not

Could not

Should not

Magnetic Letters. If you still have those magnetic letters for the fridge left over from when your child was small, get them out now and practice with contractions. (You can use a space to indicate the apostrophe, or make your own by cutting a piece of magnetized vinyl.) Practice while you're cooking in the kitchen.

Contraction Time-Out. Write a list of words that can be made into contractions (or use the magnetic letters again), and see how fast your child can call out the correct contraction. If you have enough children, form teams.

Alphabet Soup. The next time you serve alphabet soup, see if your child can find a contraction among the letters.

Contraction Hunt. Go on a "contraction hunt": Give your child a magazine or newspaper, and a brightly colored highlighter. Have her highlight every contraction she can find. If you have more than one player, set time limits for more fun.

What Tests May Ask

Standardized tests for second grade will include questions on contractions. They will be presented in two ways: They will ask children to choose the original words making up a contraction, or they will present two words and ask children to choose the correct contraction.

Practice Skill: Contractions

Directions: Choose the contraction that means the same as the given word or word pair.

Example:

is not

Ⓐ isnot

Ⓑ isn't

Ⓒ is'not

Ⓓ not

Answer:

Ⓑ isn't

---

13 did not

Ⓐ don't

Ⓑ didn't

Ⓒ can't

Ⓓ doesn't

---

14 It is

Ⓐ Its

Ⓑ It's

Ⓒ Itis

Ⓓ It isn't

---

15 I will

Ⓐ Iwill

Ⓑ I'ill

Ⓒ I'll

Ⓓ Ill

---

16 would not

Ⓐ won't

Ⓑ wouldn't

Ⓒ would'nt

Ⓓ willn't

---

17 should not

    Ⓐ shall not

    Ⓑ shld'nt

    Ⓒ should

    Ⓓ shouldn't

18 do not

    Ⓐ doesn't

    Ⓑ didn't

    Ⓒ doe'snt

    Ⓓ don't

19 cannot

    Ⓐ can't

    Ⓑ couldn't

    Ⓒ can'ot

    Ⓓ cann't

(See page 133 for the answer key.)

CHAPTER 7

Spelling

In the adult world, a person's work is often judged by its correct or incorrect spelling. Even in today's world of spellcheckers and grammar checkers, a basic ability to spell correctly is very important. While many adults proudly proclaim that they "just can't spell," the reality is that there's a big payoff to having this basic skill.

Almost all schools use some type of basic word list of common words that students are expected to master. Ask your child's teacher what list he uses, and see if you can get a copy so that you will know what words your child is learning at school. Ask your child's teacher for a copy of your state's second-grade word list. If your teacher can't provide one, you can write to the local school district office or instructional division of your state department of public instruction and ask whether there is a list. If there is, ask if they will send you a copy.

Spelling

What Second Graders Should Know

Most students who have been introduced to spelling in first grade will, by second grade, be able to spell common words. For example, when your child hears the word *kid,* he should be able to predict that the first letter is either a *c* or *k* and that the rest of the word will be made with an *i* followed by *d.*

Most children have been taught how to spell easy one- and two-syllable words in first grade. By second grade they are ready to begin learn-ing some of the more common irregularly spelled words, such as *women* and *school.* Your child also should be ready to learn common spelling rules, such as "*i* before *e,* except after *c*" and "change the *y* to *ie* and add *es.*" By this age, your second grader should be able to use more and more multi-syllable and irregularly spelled words in his daily writing.

Most second graders also should be able to begin to pick out spelling errors, which is a slightly more complicated skill than simply memorizing spelling words. At this age, your child should be able to check his writing and flag words he's not sure of so that he can look them up in the dictionary.

What You and Your Child Can Do

Spelling is one of those activities that can be easy and fun to work on at home. It doesn't have to be drudgery—no long lists of words to learn by rote! When working on spelling, however, it's best to use games that will allow your child to write the words. People don't spell out loud, except in artificial situations. Because we usually write or read words, children need to develop a visual image of words, so that they can learn the way a word looks when it is spelled right. This is one reason that spelling bees aren't the best way to learn spelling. (This also means that the worst spellers usually get the least practice.)

Play Hangman. This old favorite is a wonderful way to learn spelling words. Have your child choose a word, mark out the spaces for each letter, and then you guess the rest of the letters. Then switch, and you choose a word and let your child guess the missing letters. Give your child some helpful strategies: Suggest that he try vowels first because all words must have vowels. Ask him which letters are most common. If the second letter is an *h,* talk about what letter might go with the *h—s* or *c,* for example. You can play this game anywhere, with paper and pencil, on a chalkboard, dry erase board, or even with magnetic letters on a fridge.

Play Online Hangman. If your child is computer savvy, he can play hangman online, at the Web site http://www.nanana.com/hngmn.htm. Log on and have fun with this interactive game.

Look It Up. Get your child an inexpensive, age-appropriate dictionary, and encourage him to check the spelling of words.

Be an Editor! By second grade, children should become more accustomed to the process of editing. When your beginning second grader writes a note to Uncle Ted thanking him for the skates, have him write a rough draft, and then go over it with him for major errors. Some words are just too difficult to sound out and spell correctly. If you detect a misspelled word, see if he can come up with the correct spelling.

Spell by Touch. In general, the more senses your child uses when learning, the better your child will remember what he has learned. Try tracing a word on your child's back, and have him say the word. This is a good game for siblings or a friend to play during a sleepover.

Play Concentration. Take 10 words from your child's word list at school. Using a set of index cards, have your child print a word on each card. Print a second set and then turn all the cards over. The first player turns over 2 cards—if they match, he keeps the cards. If they don't match, he puts them back where he got them. The second player then takes a turn. As your child

becomes more adept at playing, increase the spelling words to 15.

Make Shaving Cream Letters. Cover a flat washable surface with shaving cream. Have your child trace his spelling words in the shaving cream. When finished, wipe off with a damp cloth.

Check Homework. By the middle of second grade, you should review your child's written homework and point out misspellings. Be prepared for some teachers to resist your efforts at correcting your child's spelling, but it's important that at this age you help your child get used to having written work edited. The longer we allow children to practice incorrect spelling, the more difficult it will be for them to learn the correct way.

As you edit your child's homework and the school papers that he brings home, make a list of words your child often misspells. You'll find your child will routinely misspell the same words and make the same errors (usually one or two letters) in each difficult word. Print those words on index cards, with the routinely misspelled letters in a bold color and drill him on the challenging words from time to time. For example, if he routinely misspells the word *school* as "skool," write it on the card as "**sch**ool."

Most state departments of public instruction provide lists of required (or recommended) words that children at each grade level should be able to read and spell. These lists can be a helpful resource because they are generally designed to match the vocabulary children in each grade encounter in the curriculum and the level of the vocabulary used in that state's standardized tests.

Eat Your Letters. In ancient times, mothers taught their children to spell by shaping letters out of cookie dough. After they were baked, the children would hold the letter, say the sound, then eat the letter. Try baking some letters and letting your child spell simple words—and then eat the results! No time to make dough? You can find premixed sugar cookie dough in the refrigerator section of most grocery stores.

Make a Word Pyramid. In this game, you're trying to see how many words your child can make out of one beginning word. Start him off with a simple word, such as *me*. Have him print ME on a piece of paper, or draw it on a chalk board. Then under it, add one more letter to make a word. Under each layer of the pyramid, add one more letter.

ME
MET
MEAT
STEAM
STEAMS

Use Spelling Software. Look for grade-appropriate software, such as *Spelling Blaster*. These programs provide immediate feedback and have the added advantage of presenting spelling in a nonthreatening, fun video game format that most children enjoy. If your child wants to use the family computer, visit the school and check out their software; obtain the same software if possible.

If your second grader enjoys using your adult word processing software, turn on the automatic spell flagging to help provide immediate feedback. New adult-level word processing software alerts users to misspelled words with devices such as alarm buzzes or flashing red underlines. Although these programs will flag words that they simply don't recognize (such as many proper names), they will also flag misspellings such as "I road the buse to school." (But note that the spell flaggers would typically not highlight the incorrect spelling "road" because that is a correct spelling in another context.)

Make Glow Words. A fun way to practice spelling words is to give your child glow-in-the-dark paint, pens, or crayons. Have him write his spelling words on white paper using glow-in-the-dark materials. Then hang up the words and have him enjoy reading them in the dark!

Play Scrabblin' Spell. You can use regular *Scrabble* tiles for this activity, or you can make your own letter tiles by simply cutting out squares from an index card and printing one letter in each square. Mix them up face down, and have your child pick six letters at random. Challenge him to see how many words he can spell in one minute. This is a good activity for two or more children to play on a rainy day.

What Tests May Ask

Standardized testing of spelling can't ask your child to write down spelling words; instead, he'll be asked to choose the correct spelling from a list of incorrect choices or to choose the one incorrect word from a list of possibilities. Tests will typically include difficult words that require a child to recognize the irregular use of spelling sounds, such as *sch* in school.

Practice Skill: Spelling

Directions: Choose the correctly spelled word to go into the blank.

Example:

Susan wants _____ pie.

Ⓐ sum
Ⓑ sume
Ⓒ som
Ⓓ some

Answer:

Ⓓ some

1 When I hear a joke, I _____.

Ⓐ laff

Ⓑ lauff

Ⓒ laugh

Ⓓ laughe

2 I like to read at ____.

Ⓐ skul

Ⓑ skool

Ⓒ skule

Ⓓ school

3 Sarah is my best _____.

Ⓐ freind

Ⓑ friend

Ⓒ frende

Ⓓ frend

4 I like to walk _____ the town.

Ⓐ arund

Ⓑ arounde

Ⓒ around

Ⓓ arond

Directions: Pick out the word that is spelled **incorrectly** in the sentences below.

Example:

Are you going to wear the blak dress?

Ⓐ you

Ⓑ wear

Ⓒ dress

Ⓓ blak

Answer:

Ⓓ blak

5 Ahmed told us all a really funy joke.

Ⓐ told

Ⓑ really

Ⓒ funy

Ⓓ joke

6 Harry didn't know if he wuld go to the city tomorrow.

Ⓐ didn't

Ⓑ wuld

Ⓒ city

Ⓓ tomorrow

7 Wher is the brown necklace that you took?

Ⓐ Wher

Ⓑ brown

Ⓒ necklace

Ⓓ took

(See page 133 for the answer key.)

Root Words, Suffixes, and Prefixes

Root words are the original forms of words that can be made into other words by adding a prefix or suffix. For example, the root word in *prettiest* is *pretty*. Suffixes and prefixes in the second grade involve learning about simple word endings and beginnings, and what they mean. Knowledge of *prefixes* (word beginnings) can help second graders puzzle out the meaning of a word: *pre* means before, then *prewriting* may be "what you do before you write." *Suffixes* are word endings, such as the *er* in *player,* and knowledge of these can also help a child understand a word's meaning.

What Second Graders Should Know

Most second graders should be able to recognize the term *root word* and understand its meaning because their teachers probably will use that term. Second graders also can identify common root words such as *walk* in *walking* and *big* in *biggest.*

Although many early second graders will be confused by the concepts of prefixes and suffixes, by late second grade most students will be able to identify common examples of both. In many cases they will also be able to state their meaning; for example, *er* means "one who," as in "A *player* is one who plays."

What You and Your Child Can Do

Mix and Match. To help your child work on root words, suffixes, and prefixes, print some common root words, prefixes, and suffixes on separate index cards. Lay out the cards, and have your child play "mix and match" with different endings and beginnings for the root words.

Concentration. In this version of concentration, you can take the index cards (root words, endings, and beginnings) you made in the activity above, and turn them face down. Have your child turn over two cards at a time; if the root word fits with an ending or a beginning, that's a match! Your child takes the cards and chooses again. At the end of the game, the player with the most matches wins.

What Tests May Ask

Standardized tests for the second grade will include questions on root words, suffixes, and prefixes. In some cases, students will be asked to identify the root word, prefix, or suffix from a group of given words. Some will be straightforward, such as asking the root word of *playing,* but some may be more difficult, such as asking for the root word for *riding,* a word in which the *e* has been dropped.

Practice Skill: Root Words, Prefixes, and Suffixes

Directions: What is the root word in the following underlined words?

Example:

nicest

- Ⓐ nicer
- Ⓑ nice
- Ⓒ nices
- Ⓓ nicest

Answer:

- Ⓑ nice

---

8 sweetest

- Ⓐ sweetening
- Ⓑ sweeter
- Ⓒ sweet
- Ⓓ sweeten

---

9 <u>prettiest</u>

  Ⓐ prettie

  Ⓑ prettier

  Ⓒ pretty

  Ⓓ pretties

10 <u>hopping</u>

  Ⓐ hop

  Ⓑ hoppy

  Ⓒ hoppin

  Ⓓ hopp

11 <u>sleeping</u>

  Ⓐ sleepier

  Ⓑ sleeps

  Ⓒ sleepin

  Ⓓ sleep

12 <u>meaner</u>

  Ⓐ meane

  Ⓑ meanie

  Ⓒ mean

  Ⓓ means

Directions: Identify the *suffix* in each of the following underlined words.

Example:

<u>allowing</u>

  Ⓐ allow

  Ⓑ allowin

  Ⓒ ing

  Ⓓ all

Answer:

  Ⓒ ing

13 <u>hunted</u>

  Ⓐ hunt

  Ⓑ ted

  Ⓒ ed

  Ⓓ hun

14 <u>rooted</u>

  Ⓐ ed

  Ⓑ ted

  Ⓒ root

  Ⓓ rooted

15 <u>ringing</u>

  Ⓐ ring

  Ⓑ in

  Ⓒ ing

  Ⓓ ging

16 What suffix do we add to the word <u>hunt</u> to mean "one who hunts"?

  Ⓐ er

  Ⓑ ed

  Ⓒ ted

  Ⓓ hunting

Directions: Identify the *prefix* in each of the following underlined words.

Example:

<u>bicycle</u>

Ⓐ cycle

Ⓑ bicycle

Ⓒ bi

Ⓓ cle

Answer:

Ⓒ bi

---

17 <u>preschool</u>

Ⓐ ol

Ⓑ ool

Ⓒ school

Ⓓ pre

---

18 <u>unhappy</u>

Ⓐ happy

Ⓑ un

Ⓒ py

Ⓓ ppy

---

19 <u>nonsense</u>

Ⓐ sen

Ⓑ se

Ⓒ nonsense

Ⓓ non

---

20 What does the prefix *re* mean in the word <u>rebuild</u>?

Ⓐ to knock down

Ⓑ not to build

Ⓒ to build before

Ⓓ to build again

---

21 What does the prefix *un* mean in the word <u>unfair</u>?

Ⓐ fair

Ⓑ not fair

Ⓒ sometimes fair

Ⓓ fair again

(See pages 133–134 for the answer key.)

CHAPTER 8

Capitalization and Punctuation

As children enter second grade, they are introduced in a much more formal way to the mysteries of capitalization and punctuation marks. Capitalizing proper nouns is one of the first skills children learn in second grade. They learn that titles of books, movies, computer games and software, songs, and TV programs all begin with capital letters, as do the names of people, towns, states, addresses, and so on.

Capitalization

What Second Graders Should Know

In kindergarten and first grade, your child's teachers have probably emphasized capitalization and punctuation in isolation. This approach changes in second grade, however, as your child's teacher begins to teach students that sentences begin with capital letters. At first your child may have trouble figuring out when sentences actually begin, and she may capitalize the first letter of the first word following a comma or the first letter at the beginning of every line.

By late second grade, however, your child should be able to choose which nouns to capitalize and to apply these principles to longer passages that she reads and writes. She will gradually develop a greater appreciation for the rules that govern when and where to use these language devices. By capitalizing and punctuating correctly, readers will be given a guideline to better understand your child's writing.

This is not as easy as it may seem, however. Your second grader may mix up the rules about which letters in titles *not* to capitalize (as in *Junie B. Jones and the Yucky Blucky Fruitcake*). At first she may find it hard to tell the difference between proper nouns and other nouns, and she may mistakenly capitalize all nouns in sentences (such as "My Dog Baxter ran down the Street"). By the end of second grade, your child should understand which nouns require capitalization.

What You and Your Child Can Do

The best way for children to learn capitalization is to practice writing as often as possible. By second grade, most children can benefit from gentle correction when they make a basic capitalization error. There are lots of ways you can get your child to practice.

Write a Story. Have your child write a story about a favorite hobby or experience, and go over it gently, pointing out glaring capitalization mistakes (such as not capitalizing the pronoun *I,* names of people, or the first word of a sentence).

Take a Letter! Writing the addresses on envelopes is good practice for capitalization rules. During second grade, don't miss an opportunity to let your child help you address holiday cards and invitations. Encourage her to write a letter to a hero, favorite author, political leader, sports figure, musician, or athlete. Make sure all the capital letters are correct in the address.

Be an Editor for a Day. Many children even as young as first or second grade love to work on the computer. Write a story in a paragraph or two, and make it as funny as you can. Include lots of capitalization errors, and then let your child edit the paragraph on the computer.

What Tests May Ask

Because current standardized tests must assess capitalization skills in a way that can be scored by computer, they must rely on a child's ability to *recognize* correct capitalization rather than produce it. As a result, standardized tests today ask fairly straightforward questions about capitalization.

Some computer-assisted testing procedures are now being developed that will allow children to enter their responses so that computers can assess *expressive* capitalization skills, but these aren't widely available now.

Practice Skill: Capitalization

Directions: Read these sentences. Then choose the words that need to begin with capital letters.

Example:

For our vacation, we are going to new jersey.

ⓐ our
ⓑ vacation
ⓒ going
ⓓ new jersey

Answer:

ⓓ new jersey

1 we will be going to the park tomorrow.

ⓐ we
ⓑ will
ⓒ park
ⓓ tomorrow

2 Rosita gave her cake to peter.

ⓐ gave
ⓑ her
ⓒ cake
ⓓ peter

3 The band will play their concert on friday.

ⓐ band
ⓑ play
ⓒ concert
ⓓ friday

4 You and i must go to the library.

ⓐ i
ⓑ must
ⓒ go
ⓓ library

5 On the fifth of march, we all went to the market.

ⓐ fifth
ⓑ march
ⓒ went
ⓓ market

6 suddenly the sailboat turned over in the lake.

   Ⓐ suddenly

   Ⓑ sailboat

   Ⓒ turned

   Ⓓ lake

Directions: Choose the letter beneath the error in each sentence.

Example:

When mr. Smith came, we helped
   Ⓐ Ⓑ Ⓒ

him unpack.
     Ⓓ

Answer:

   Ⓑ mr.

7 We can expect lots of turkey at
  Ⓐ   Ⓑ   Ⓒ

thanksgiving.
   Ⓓ

8 are you leaving for Italy for a
  Ⓐ Ⓑ   Ⓒ

vacation on Tuesday?
         Ⓓ

9 Sarah says she will take Chip to
  Ⓐ   Ⓑ

see dr. Smith.
   Ⓒ Ⓓ

10 Are You going to church on
  Ⓐ Ⓑ   Ⓒ

Sunday?
  Ⓓ

Directions: Choose the sentence that shows correct capitalization.

Example:

   Ⓐ Carlitos and Cindy are Going to town today.

   Ⓑ Are you going to make a Pineapple cake?

   Ⓒ On Tuesday, we will both go to Paris.

   Ⓓ where are you?

Answer:

   Ⓒ On Tuesday, we will both go to Paris.

11 Ⓐ In the Winter, Jake likes to go skiing.

   Ⓑ I don't like Chocolate Chip cookies for lunch.

   Ⓒ Christie is going to move to Southern pennsylvania.

   Ⓓ My favorite holiday comes in December.

12 Ⓐ Our little Dog is a Golden retriever.

   Ⓑ Will you come to visit us in our new house in Arizona?

   Ⓒ At Midnight, the dog began to howl.

   Ⓓ We like to carve Pumpkins on Halloween.

13 Ⓐ blake doesn't always brush his teeth.

Ⓑ Spot, my Dog, likes to chase his tail.

Ⓒ My favorite book is Peter pan.

Ⓓ I live at 314 Red School Road.

14 Ⓐ I'm going to write a thank you note to Aunt Alice.

Ⓑ mom, can I go to the fair?

Ⓒ Mohammed told his friend john that he could not go.

Ⓓ Debbie likes to sing tunes from The sound of music.

(See page 134 for the answer key.)

Punctuation

The first punctuation mark that children learn is the period to mark the end of a sentence. First-grade teachers don't usually stress punctuation because they are more concerned with helping children get used to putting their thoughts down on paper. In second grade, however, your child will find the teacher places far more emphasis on punctuation, which will probably include the period, question mark, exclamation point, and comma.

Up to now, your child probably wrote stories and reports in one long sentence or paragraph, not able to distinguish where one idea stopped and another began. She also may have read a story in the same way, as if it were all one big run-on sentence, with no pause for breath or intonation.

What Second Graders Should Know

By second grade, you should begin to see your child start to use more sophisticated methods of punctuating thoughts and sentences. Second graders may not have consistent control over punctuation, but they show their understanding by incorporating all the commonly used punctuation marks to some degree in their writing. By the end of the year, they should be using periods to end simple sentences, approximate the use of quotation marks, use exclamation marks for emphasis, and use question marks.

Periods

By second grade, your child should be able to easily identify where to put periods in simple, declarative sentences such as "Sarah likes to ride horseback. Tom likes to play football."

Question Marks

The next punctuation mark children in second grade learn is the question mark. While most first-grade teachers mention that question marks go at the end of a sentence that asks a question, they usually don't require children to use these marks themselves.

By second grade, children are usually quite comfortable with question marks—it's very easy to tell which sentences are statements and which ask questions—and many teachers therefore require them.

Exclamation Marks

Most early elementary school youngsters are an enthusiastic lot, and it shows in their essays, which tend to be filled with exclamation marks. At this age, almost every sentence is an exclamatory one. This tendency to overuse exclamation marks continues in second grade, but by the end of the year—as your child becomes experienced in writing and with life in general—her writing will gradually become less breathless with exuberance.

Commas

Many second graders still find commas confusing—and let's face it, so do many adults. Most teachers are content in second grade to emphasize simple comma use, and by the end of second grade they may begin to teach comma use in a series. However, the distinction between when it's appropriate to use a comma or a semicolon is beyond the ken of most second graders.

Instead, expect your child's teacher to discuss the use of commas between several items in a list, in dates, and in greetings in personal letters.

What You and Your Child Can Do

Write to a Pen Pal. Ask your child to write a postcard to Aunt Sharon telling her about the fishing trip you just went on during vacation. Go over your child's first "sloppy copy" to check for punctuation mistakes, and then let her copy the words onto a postcard. Or have her write a postcard to her pet, and mail it to her home address. (This is a great way to keep track of vacations; if you save these cards, after 20 years, you'll have wonderful vacation memories, in addition to giving your child writing practice!)

Read Aloud. One way to help remind your child to focus on punctuation is to have her read her work out loud. If your child seems to be having trouble with punctuation, get her to read to you a paragraph that she's written. When she does this, it's much more obvious where the sentence should end with a period, or where a pause would indicate a comma. It just *sounds* right. Remind her that if she's not sure about punctuation, she should read the sentence to herself quietly to see if that helps steer her in the right direction.

Keep a Diary. Encourage your child to keep a diary. There are great-looking journals and diaries at stationery stores and bookstores, and they make nice gifts for children. Keeping a diary will give your child a chance to get used to writing down her feelings and experiences. Don't worry yet about sophisticated colons, semicolons, dashes, quotation marks, and ellipses. For now, just have her concentrate on periods, question marks, and exclamation points—that's what the standardized tests will focus on as well.

The Editor Is In. This activity works just as well for punctuation as for capitalization: Write a funny story on your computer, and put in lots of punctuation errors. Tell your child how many errors she should look for (it's less frustrating for children if you tell them how many mistakes there are).

What Tests May Ask

Because standardized tests must be given in a format that will allow answer sheets to be scored by computer, the questions test a child's ability to *recognize* correct and incorrect punctuation when she sees it. Tests may present a choice of sentences and ask which one is punctuated correctly, or they may provide a sentence with several possibilities for punctuation and ask the child to choose where to place the period, comma, question mark, or exclamation mark.

Practice Skill: Punctuation

Directions: Choose the sentence that shows correct punctuation.

Example:

- Ⓐ Sarah, come right here?
- Ⓑ Look out!
- Ⓒ How old are you.
- Ⓓ Sarah ran down the hill

Answer:

- Ⓑ Look out!

---

15 Ⓐ Can Weng come out to play?
 Ⓑ Look, here, I don't want to see, that.
 Ⓒ Were you going to tell her!
 Ⓓ What shall we do today.

---

16 Ⓐ How far is it to Paris.

Ⓑ Susan and Paul can, read chapter three?

Ⓒ Kara, how are you doing today?

Ⓓ The car, is going to hit us.

---

17 Ⓐ John Susan and Tom went to the park.

Ⓑ What kind of dog is that.

Ⓒ Sally, can you ride a bike!

Ⓓ Jim, will you please take your plate?

---

18 Ⓐ Bill Larry and Sue are going to school together.

Ⓑ Will you hurry up!

Ⓒ Are you going to the fair.

Ⓓ Jane please read the book.

(See page 134 for the answer key.)

Practice Skill: Capitalization and Punctuation Together

Directions: Read the following para-graph. Below each underlined phrase is a number that belongs to a ques-tion that follows. Choose the num-bered phrase that is correctly capital-ized and punctuated.

The Wind in the Willows
By Kenneth Grahame

"But what I wanted to ask you was, won't you take me to call on <u>Mr. Toad?</u>
EX.
I've heard so much about <u>him and</u> I
19
do so want to make his acquaintance."

"Why, certainly," said the good-natured Rat, jumping to his feet and dismissing poetry from his mind for the day. "Get the boat <u>out and</u> we'll
20
paddle up there at once. It's never the wrong time to call on Toad. Early or late he's always the same fellow. <u>always good-tempered always</u> glad to
21
see you, always sorry when you go!"

"<u>he must</u> be a very nice animal,"
22
observed the Mole, as he got into the boat and took the sculls, while the Rat settled himself comfortably in the <u>stern.</u>
23

Example:

Ⓐ Mr. Toad?

Ⓑ Mr. Toad.

Ⓒ Mr. Toad!

Ⓓ Mr. Toad,

Answer:

Ⓐ Mr. Toad?

19
  Ⓐ him And
  Ⓑ him, and
  Ⓒ Him, and
  Ⓓ Him And

20
  Ⓐ out and
  Ⓑ out, and
  Ⓒ Out, and
  Ⓓ out, And

21
  Ⓐ always good-tempered always
  Ⓑ always good-tempered, always
  Ⓒ always, good-tempered always
  Ⓓ Always good-tempered, always

22
  Ⓐ "He must
  Ⓑ "he Must
  Ⓒ "He, must
  Ⓓ "he must

23
  Ⓐ Stern
  Ⓑ stern
  Ⓒ stern.
  Ⓓ stern?"

(See page 134 for the answer key.)

CHAPTER 9

Grammar Skills

By the time they are in second grade, most children have become fairly sophisticated in their ability to speak and write correctly. They've learned many of the rules they need to know to write correctly in a fluent and expressive manner. Grammar skills include being able to recognize and use correctly the regular and irregular nouns, verbs, and adjectives, as well as the possessive forms of pronouns and sentence construction.

Parts of Speech

What Second Graders Should Know

Your child is now learning to speak and write effectively. He will have learned that some words have both regular and irregular uses, and he can generalize the rules of the English language. He'll know what pronouns are, and how to make them possessive. By second grade, most children will have learned that many verbs don't follow the regular rules for the present and past tenses.

But language expression is more than a collection of nouns and verbs. By the middle to late second grade, most children are able to understand the building blocks of written expression, so that they can judge when simple sentences are formed correctly and pick out incorrect or misplaced elements. This means that most second graders understand the English formula of noun-verb-object: "Sam jumped over the log." Most will be able to identify mistakes in word order: "Sam the log jumped."

Nouns

By this age, your child knows that nouns are the name of a person, place, or thing. He can read a story and pick out all the nouns, or write the nouns next to a picture. He can also form plurals of most nouns simply by adding an *s:* one horse, two horses. Second graders should be able to generalize this rule to include a wide variety of nouns.

At the same time, they will become aware that many nouns in our language don't follow this simple rule: You have one goose but two geese, one army but two armies. On the other hand, your second grader may be surprised to learn that not all words change from singular to plural: one deer, two deer, 500 deer.

Once they understand simple plurals, second graders then move on to learn how to show possession. Most children this age will be able to understand that for most nouns, a simple apostrophe and an *s* will show possession (John's book). Only in later years will children learn the irregularities of this rule (for example, a noun ending in an *s* sound can be made possessive by adding an apostrophe alone—Dennis' hat).

Pronouns

Many second graders find the term *pronoun* confusing. They learn that the term refers to nouns that stand for other nouns. By second grade children learn the masculine and feminine pronouns, plural pronouns, and neutral pronouns. Possessive pronouns are also on a second grader's syllabus: Ryan looked for his favorite video to give to Emily for her birthday.

Verbs

Most second graders get the hang of verbs (*action words* or "doing" words)—but choosing the correct form may be more tricky. Tenses are also important, and your child is learning how to use the right tense of a verb in a sentence. The simple rules, such as the formation of past tense by adding *ed,* have been easily mastered, but many younger children still tend to extrapolate the rules to every verb: "I goed to the store." The more sophisticated second graders will figure out that some of the more common verbs don't follow regular rules for present and past tense: *Bring* in the present tense becomes *brought* in the past. Most second graders will be able to begin to learn which common verbs follow regular rules for present and past tense and which are irregular. Second graders will also learn irregular verbs that tell when something is happening now—*is, are,* and *am.* They also learn how to make nouns and verbs agree in the present tense—for example, "I sing," but "she sings."

Adjectives

While your child may have found adjectives confusing in the past, by second grade he has probably mastered simple adjectives. Once he has done so, he can move on to learn how to make comparative forms by adding *er* or *est* to regular adjectives to describe something as being "more than" or the superlative "most." Irregular adjectives may still trip up a typical second grader, who may forget that if one piece of candy is good, two is better. Over time, however, he can learn the correct forms by simple repetition; eventually he will be able to choose the correct form simply because it "sounds right."

What You and Your Child Can Do

Read! Throughout second grade, you should continue doing what you have been doing for some time to help teach your child the grammar of his language—reading to him. As you read from a wide variety of books in areas that interest you both, your child is exposed to the correct grammatical form of vivid language.

Match Pictures and Actions. Have your child cut out from magazines some pictures that can be described with nouns, and paste the pictures onto index cards. Then have him print a noun on individual index cards. Have your child match the appropriate noun with a picture.

Play the Match Game. Using the cards you made in the preceding activity, arrange matching sets (such as a picture of a baby crying and the word *cry*) face down in rows. The first player turns over two cards, trying to match the noun with the verb. If he is successful, he gets to keep the two matching cards and take another turn. If he is unsuccessful, he returns the cards face down. The player with the most cards at the end wins.

Talk and Listen. Reading isn't the only way to reinforce the rules of language usage. In everyday conversation, you can reinforce proper grammar in subtle ways so that your child automatically learns the correct patterns of grammatical English. Learning proper grammar in the beginning is much easier than later having to unlearn improper or sloppy language usage.

Teachers work very hard in school to develop their students' English skills, but if English is a child's native language, the odds are that the patterns he learns at home are the ones he knows best and is most comfortable with. This is why it's so important for parents to use correct English and to model good language skills for their children.

Remember that to foster good English usage habits, you must also listen to your child. Second graders are eager to describe everyday events and to share with you their hopes and dreams. Invite your second grader to join in the conversation around the family table.

Make a Grammar Collage. Have your child cut out from magazines pictures that can be described with nouns and then other pictures that can be described with verbs. Now have him paste the pictures together to make a grammar collage.

Play Computer Games. A host of computer games can help foster good grammatical skills through fun practice. *Kid Works Deluxe* (Davidson) encourages youngsters to create multimedia books, stories, poems, and more using words together with pictures and sounds. In *Grammar Games* (Davidson), kids can engage in four exciting rain forest activities as they solve problems of plurals and possessives, identify noun-verb agreements, edit sentences for proper verb usage, and recognize sentence fragments. The game includes a complete language guide that provides grammar rules and examples at the click of the mouse.

Start a Journal. At this age, it can be helpful to give your child suggestions on topics to write about in his journal: What would your daily life be like if you were 4 inches tall? If you could be any sort of animal, what would you be? For those children who enjoy writing in their journals, the extra practice in grammatical skills will really pay off. If your child is reluctant to write in his journal at night, write down a question for him to explore (What would life be like if you lived at the bottom of the ocean?). Seal the question in an envelope, and don't let him open it until he's crawled under the covers at night with his journal. Then let him spend an "extra" 10 minutes past his bedtime quietly writing a response.

Write Silly Stories. Here's an activity that youngsters just seem to love. Jot down a brief story, leaving blanks in crucial spots where words are left out. Without revealing what the story is about, ask your child to give you words that you'll use to fill in the story blanks. You'll ask for adjectives, nouns, verbs, or pronouns— sometimes a blank may require a plural form. As your child offers words, jot them down. Then read the story with the words in the blanks.

Here's an example of what a story of blanks might look like:

One day the <u>NOUN</u> jumped into his <u>ADJECTIVE</u> convertible <u>NOUN</u> and drove off with his <u>ADJECTIVE</u> dog.

Your child might give the following parts of speech that you've asked for:

1. pickle
2. squishy
3. cat
4. grumpy

The story would then be read:

One day the <u>PICKLE</u> jumped into his <u>SQUISHY</u> convertible <u>CAT</u> and drove off with his <u>GRUMPY</u> dog.

Have Children Share Their Writing. A fun activity, especially if your child has a friend over or you have several children near the same age, is to develop an ongoing story. This can be effective composed on a computer or simply written by hand. Have one child start off a story and break off after a few sentences; then have the second child continue. Then the first child picks up the tale, and so on. Have them pay special attention to parts of speech as they work on the story.

Read and Write Poetry. One of the best ways to broaden your child's use of adjectives is to work with poetry—reading poetry is effective, but having your child come up with his own is even better. Most children will need a bit of help, however. Try this writing exercise to jump-start the adjective flow:

————, ————, —————— puppies,

————, ————, —————— puppies,
Puppies, puppies, puppies.

Give your child a letter to start—let's say the letter *c*. Then he must come up with three adjectives beginning with *c* to describe the puppies— *cuddly, cute, curly haired, charming, cushiony.*

Encourage creativity, and watch what happens! You can use as many verses as you want and change the subject to something of interest to your child.

Dear Author... To get your child to practice writing skills, have your child write a letter of appreciation to his favorite author or illustrator, explaining why he likes a particular book. Check the letter for correct grammar and usage, and make gentle corrections if necessary.

What Tests May Ask

Second-grade teachers usually assess how well a child understands the right way to use parts of speech by grading written essays and by having children fill in blanks or provide short answers to questions.

Unfortunately, most standardized tests today assess grammar skills by testing a child's ability to *recognize* correct usage. On such a test, a child reads a sentence and then chooses the grammatically correct answer for the blank. Recognizing correct usage is much easier for a child to do than trying to come up with the correct part of speech or usage on his own.

Practice Skill: Parts of Speech

Directions: Read the following sentences, and choose the correct noun to go in the blank.

Example:

Sarah lost her book. "Did you see _____ book?" her friend Tim asked their teacher.

Ⓐ Sarahs

Ⓑ Sarahes

Ⓒ Sarah

Ⓓ Sarah's

Answer:

Ⓓ Sarah's

---

1 There was one girl in the class. There were three ____ in the hall.

Ⓐ girlses

Ⓑ girl

Ⓒ girl's

Ⓓ girls

---

2 Susan found a pack of wild _____ in the street.

Ⓐ dog's

Ⓑ dogs

Ⓒ dogs'

Ⓓ doggs

---

3 I never saw so many pretty _____!

Ⓐ hats

Ⓑ hat's

Ⓒ hats'

Ⓓ hatses

---

4 There were two _____ by the side of the road.

Ⓐ deers

Ⓑ deer

Ⓒ deers'

Ⓓ deeres

Directions: Read each sentence, and choose the letter underneath the noun.

Example:

He ate cake today.

Ⓐ   Ⓑ   Ⓒ   Ⓓ

- Ⓐ   He
- Ⓑ   ate
- Ⓒ   cake
- Ⓓ   today

Answer:

- Ⓒ   cake

---

5   Peggy took her dog to the beach.

     Ⓐ   Ⓑ   Ⓒ   Ⓓ

- Ⓐ   took
- Ⓑ   her
- Ⓒ   dog
- Ⓓ   the

Directions: Read the sentences below, and choose the correct pronoun to fill in the blank.

Example: George looked under his bed, but ___ could not find his puppy.

- Ⓐ   he
- Ⓑ   his
- Ⓒ   him
- Ⓓ   it

Answer:

- Ⓐ   he

6   Sharon made ____ bed.

- Ⓐ   she
- Ⓑ   its
- Ⓒ   her
- Ⓓ   hers

---

7   Although he was hungry, Sam did not eat ___ lunch.

- Ⓐ   he
- Ⓑ   she
- Ⓒ   hers
- Ⓓ   his

Directions: Read each sentence. Then choose the correct pronoun to fit in the blank.

Example:

Pedro likes to eat pizza. _____ likes pizza.

- Ⓐ   She
- Ⓑ   He
- Ⓒ   Her
- Ⓓ   Him

Answer:

- Ⓑ   He

---

8   Cassie is a very good artist. _____ is a very good artist.

- Ⓐ   She
- Ⓑ   Her
- Ⓒ   He
- Ⓓ   Him

9 Francesca and Betsy love to dance. _____ love to dance.

    Ⓐ Hers

    Ⓑ They

    Ⓒ Their

    Ⓓ She

10 Miranda and Cho like to skate. They wear _____ own skates.

    Ⓐ her

    Ⓑ his

    Ⓒ yours

    Ⓓ their

Directions: Choose the sentence that is written correctly.

Example:

    Ⓐ Simon wented to bed early.

    Ⓑ I seen our teacher in the store.

    Ⓒ Susan and Tom goed to church together.

    Ⓓ Sherry went to town alone.

Answer:

    Ⓓ Sherry went to town alone.

11 Ⓐ My dog like to dig in the garden.

    Ⓑ Energy make things work.

    Ⓒ He come to town every day.

    Ⓓ Alissa saw the movie yesterday.

(See page 134 for the answer key.)

Sentences

A *sentence* is a group of words that tells a complete idea, and it must include both a noun and a verb.

What Second Graders Should Know

In second grade, students are learning the correct sequence of sentences, and they should be able to produce coherent, complete sentences. They also should be able to identify sentences that aren't grammatically correct. Children this age should learn that a sentence must begin with a capital letter and must have a "stop sign" at the end—some type of end punctuation.

What You and Your Child Can Do

Sentence Match Up. This simple game is a good way to help your child learn to construct good sentences. First, write individual words on index cards (be sure to include some nouns, adjectives, pronouns, and verbs). For nouns, you can also paste pictures from magazines on cards. Then mix the cards, and have your child rearrange them to make up sentences.

Reading. Learning correct sentence structure is made much easier the more that a child is exposed to correctly worded sentences. Let your child read to you, but also be sure to read to your child every day. When you read to your second grader, choose a book that is a bit too hard for him to read himself. Exposing your child to a slightly more challenging book is another good way to improve his grammar skills.

Sentence Substitutes. On a pad of Post-its, write the pronouns your child has learned (such as *I, me, hers, his*). Then on a blackboard or dry erase board, print a sentence in large letters, such as: David went to the store. Ask your child to read the sentence out loud and then reread it substituting a pronoun for "David." The Post-it note should be placed over the word "David" and then read again. Take turns making up sentences and attaching Post-it pronouns.

Sentence Stretchers. Here's a good way to get your children thinking in creative ways when it comes to writing sentences. On 10 slips of paper write down 10 different verbs, one on each slip. Next write 10 nouns. Finally, take 4 slips of paper and write down each of these words: *when, where, why,* and *how.* The first player then draws a slip from the noun pile and a slip from the verb pile, and then one of the four *when-where-why-how* words. For example, a player drew the words *banana* and *glow* and the *when-where* word *why,* he would write: "The banana glows because he's happy."

What Tests May Ask

Standardized tests in the second grade may present a list of sentences and ask a child to choose the correct one. Incorrect sentences may have punctuation in the wrong place or no punctuation at all (run-on sentences). Students also may be given a list of sentences from which they are asked to select the incorrect one.

Practice Skill: Sentences

Directions: Choose the sentence that is written correctly.

Example:

- Ⓐ My dog Sammie is pretty, but that dog is prettier, and Karen's dog is the prettiest of all.
- Ⓑ It's cold than it was yesterday, but not as colder as it will be tomorrow.
- Ⓒ This game is hardest than I thought it would be.
- Ⓓ This candy is good, but that one is gooder.

Answer:

- Ⓐ My dog Sammie is pretty, but that dog is prettier, and Karen's dog is the prettiest of all.

12 Ⓐ Sam ball the took.
    Ⓑ Pool in Sara swam the.
    Ⓒ I think the pretty blue is dress.
    Ⓓ My birthday is tomorrow.

13 Ⓐ Did Cunio call mother his?
    Ⓑ What time is over class?
    Ⓒ Oh, I spilled my milk.
    Ⓓ Justin song the sang.

14 Ⓐ Why do horses run they were afraid.
    Ⓑ Birds fly. South in winter it gets cold then.
    Ⓒ Hats come in all colors I like. Red hats best.
    Ⓓ I like to ride in planes. They fly high in the sky.

15 Ⓐ Bears sleep in caves they wake in spring.
    Ⓑ Her eyes are blue. They are very pretty.
    Ⓒ I wear a cape that. Keeps me warm.
    Ⓓ Joy likes jokes Kiko likes jokes too.

16 Ⓐ How many cookies do you have? I have nine.

Ⓑ Peter's cat had six. Kittens in one litter.

Ⓒ Jim likes steak Sally likes lemonade.

Ⓓ In the circus there are lions clowns make me laugh

(See page 134 for the answer key.)

CHAPTER 10

Breaking It Down

The ability to read and fully understand the content involves a host of high-level cognitive skills. Those skills include being able to pick out the important details of a story such as the main idea, the setting for the story, and the sequence of events.

As their ability to read independently develops, children in second grade can begin to more fully appreciate the fine points of literature, such as development of the main idea and the buildup of suspense. They will also more readily appreciate the sequence of events in nonfiction such as historians' descriptions of the American colonies' defeat of the British in the American Revolution. In later grades, their ability to appreciate character and plot development will continue to grow.

If your child has trouble keeping all this information straight, try helping her use a *hand map:*

THUMB:	WHO was the story about?
INDEX FINGER:	WHAT was the main problem?
MIDDLE FINGER:	WHERE did the story happen?
RING FINGER:	WHEN did the story happen?
PINKY FINGER:	HOW does the problem get solved?

Main Idea

The most important idea in a paragraph, a chapter, or a book is the *main idea.* It may be clearly stated, or the reader may have to figure it out from the information given. Learning how to sum up the main idea of a paragraph, chapter, or story is a challenging but important task for second graders.

One way to help your child learn this skill is to focus first on titles, which should sum up the entire story in a few words and predict what will be happening. The ability to provide a title for a story is important because it's closely related to the ability to understand the main idea.

What Second Graders Should Know

Second graders will find it extremely challenging to sum up an entire story—or even a single chapter—in just a few words. And yet this skill is vital as your child progresses through school.

Younger readers will at best understand a sentence or at most a paragraph at a time, but most second graders are developmentally mature enough to understand a passage's main idea. During second grade, your child will also begin to develop the ability to come up with alternate titles for the stories she reads or watches on TV. The ability to provide a title for their stories requires relatively sophisticated reading comprehension skills that generally begin only at about second grade.

What You and Your Child Can Do

Get Ready! Before starting to read a book together, spend some time talking about the main idea of the book with your child. First check out the title: Ask her for her opinion about what the book might be about. In *Five Little Peppers and How They Grew,* do we have a story about vegetables? Once your child realizes that "Peppers" is the characters' last name, the main idea should be quite clear. Then move on to the chapter titles. Ask your child if she can figure out what a chapter might be about by reading its title. What other titles might she come up with?

Alternate Titles. To boost your child's ability to summarize the main idea, brainstorm for alternate titles of story classics. Make them as funny as you want, but aim for a good summary of the story. Or choose a book without chapter titles, and have your child come up with her own.

What Tests May Ask

Standardized tests for second graders will include some questions devoted to figuring out the main idea of a passage. Questions may ask a student to choose a main idea sentence, the best title, or a topic statement that describes the passage.

Students also may be asked to choose supporting details that describe the main idea of a passage. When answering questions about the main idea, students should read the title and the passage very carefully. This will help them decode the main idea.

Practice Skill: Main Idea

Directions: Read the following story and then answer the questions.

Measuring Time

In ancient times people did not have clocks. They used the sun, moon, and seasons to tell time. When the sun rose, it was time to get up and work. When the sun set, it was time to go to bed. When the moon went around the earth one time, it was a month. As the seasons changed, people could tell when a year had passed.

Example:

To measure when a year had passed, people in ancient times

Ⓐ planted corn.

Ⓑ watched the sun.

Ⓒ watched the moon.

Ⓓ kept track of changing seasons.

Answer:

Ⓓ kept track of changing seasons.

---

1 What is this passage mostly about?

Ⓐ how fast the sun sets

Ⓑ when wristwatches were invented

Ⓒ how ancient people measured time

Ⓓ what time the sun rises

2 How did people in ancient times know it was time to get out of bed in the morning?

Ⓐ They watched for the sun to set.

Ⓑ The rising of the sun woke them.

Ⓒ Their alarm clocks woke them.

Ⓓ The sound of the rooster's crowing woke them.

3 How did people in ancient times know when a month had passed?

Ⓐ They turned over a new calendar page.

Ⓑ They watched the sun.

Ⓒ They watched the moon.

Ⓓ They noticed the seasons had changed.

4 What would another good title for this passage be?

Ⓐ Clocks and Their Uses

Ⓑ Ancient Ways to Tell Time

Ⓒ Sun and Moon

Ⓓ For Every Season

Dinosaur Dining

Dinosaurs ate many different kinds of things. Some dinosaurs ate nothing but plants. They liked flowers, leaves, ferns, and water plants. Other dinosaurs were meat eaters. They even ate other dinosaurs. Small meat-eating dinosaurs consumed bird and dinosaur eggs and smaller animals.

5 What is the main idea of the passage?

Ⓐ Smaller dinosaurs ate eggs.

Ⓑ Dinosaurs had a hard time getting food.

Ⓒ Dinosaurs liked to fight each other.

Ⓓ Dinosaurs liked to eat many kinds of food.

6 What kinds of plants did some dinosaurs eat?

Ⓐ hay and straw

Ⓑ leaves, ferns, flowers, and water plants

Ⓒ oats and alfalfa

Ⓓ cereal

7 The passage says: "Small meat-eating dinosaurs <u>consumed</u> bird and dinosaur eggs." What does <u>consumed</u> mean in this sentence?

Ⓐ ate

Ⓑ cooked

Ⓒ hid

Ⓓ carried

8 Choose the sentence that should come first in the following paragraph?

_____. All the farmers on the kibbutz share land and work together as a family. Everyone eats together in a big dining room. The children live together in a separate house. Parents and children get together after work and for holidays.

Ⓐ   Israel is a very old land.

Ⓑ   A kibbutz is a special kind of farm in Israel.

Ⓒ   All kinds of food are available.

Ⓓ   Corn tastes good.

(See page 134 for the answer key.)

Sequence

Having the ability to understand the sequence in a piece of writing means that you can figure out what comes first, next, and last in a story. It requires the abilities to determine the main idea and supporting details and the ability to retell stories.

What Second Graders Should Know

Beginning second graders should understand that events occur in a sequence, and they should be able to differentiate between first, next, and last. By the end of the year, second-grade writers should have moved beyond simply describing a sequence of events to explaining a clustering of memorable events, problems and solutions, and a main idea.

What You and Your Child Can Do

Play Title Scramble. After you finish reading a favorite book, write down each chapter title on a slip of paper. Mix them up, and ask your child to see if she can put the titles back in correct order within one minute.

Sing a Book. After reading a book with your second grader, see if you can create a song together that tells the main points of the book. Let's say you've read *The Wizard of Oz*. List a few of the main points—Dorothy lands on the Wicked Witch, meets the Scarecrow and the Lion, and goes to Oz to find the Wizard. She gets captured and then kills the witch, her friends get their wishes, and she goes home to Kansas. Make up a tune (or use an old favorite), and weave these points into the song.

Cook with Your Child. If ever there is an activity that requires things to be done in certain steps, it's cooking. Find your child's favorite (simple) recipe—or use a child's cookbook—and whip up something special together. Let your child take the lead in following the steps—try not to jump in! You'll be surprised at what may be accomplished.

Play Comic Strip Scramble. Cut up a few weeks' worth of some comic strips. (You can laminate them if you wish.) Then mix them up, and have your child put them in correct sequence. What comes first? Next? Last?

Make a Scrapbook. Nothing fascinates a second grader more than herself, so let her make a scrapbook of her life, with old birthday cards, artwork, photos, old programs and tickets, and so on. Let her add captions or narratives—chapter headings are great too!

What Tests May Ask

Standardized tests that assess sequencing ability may ask students to figure out how sentences are related to each other, or they may ask questions about the sequence of events in the passage—perhaps what the main character did and in what order.

To do well, students should remember to first scan the passage to get an idea of what the story is about before answering questions. In questions focusing on sequence, students should be alert for signal words such as *first, later, after, then, finally,* and *at last.*

Practice Skill: Sequence

Directions: Read the passage below. Then choose the best answer to each of the questions.

Latisha decided that she wanted to bake some chocolate chip cookies. What a surprise it would be for Mom! She didn't cook as well as her big sister Cindy, but tomorrow was her mother's birthday. Latisha wanted to do something special for Mom.

    First she got out the cookbook. She would need a lot of ingredients! She got out the chips, flour, butter, and milk. Next, she mixed them all together. Plop! She dropped each cookie onto the cookie sheet. Once the oven was hot enough, she popped the cookies in and set the timer.

Example:

What did Latisha want to bake?
- Ⓐ meat loaf
- Ⓑ cake
- Ⓒ bread
- Ⓓ cookies

Answer:
- Ⓓ cookies

9 What did Latisha do first in the story?
- Ⓐ put the cookies in the oven
- Ⓑ got out the cookbook
- Ⓒ got out the ingredients
- Ⓓ ate the cookies

10 Why did she want to make cookies?
- Ⓐ She wanted to make them for her mother's birthday.
- Ⓑ She wanted to make them for her school party.
- Ⓒ She liked cookies.
- Ⓓ She was hungry.

11 How was Latisha different from Cindy?
- Ⓐ She liked to cook.
- Ⓑ She liked to eat cookies.
- Ⓒ She was older than Cindy.
- Ⓓ She didn't cook as well as her older sister Cindy.

12 The story uses the word *ingredients*. What does the word *ingredients* mean in this passage?
- Ⓐ types of cookie
- Ⓑ courage
- Ⓒ energy
- Ⓓ things used to make cookies

Characters and Settings

A good book is rich in details about the characters who people its pages and the environment in which they live. Characters and setting are two of the important elements of literature.

Caring about a character makes us care about the story itself, and being able to empathize with characters and understand their motivation is central to enjoying what we read. Likewise, an interesting or compelling setting adds immeasurably to our enjoyment of what we read.

What Second Graders Should Know

By second grade, most children have begun to note details about their favorite stories, such as the setting and the time in which the story takes place. They should be able to understand more complex details about characters as well, such as the relationships among the characters, as well as their motives and moods. They can perceive details about a character's height, build, likes, dislikes, and actions if the writer discusses them and they have a bearing on the story.

Although she may tend to see characters only in terms of bad and good, your child will gradually begin to understand that bad characters aren't all bad and that good characters have flaws. Just as she begins to see people around her in an increasingly complex way, she will gradually be able to extend those skills to her reading.

For example, she may read about Robin Hood, and understand that he was a notorious highwayman who robbed from the rich to feed the poor during hard times in Great Britain. She will be able to see that rather than being a one-sided bad guy, Robin had good points—and could be considered a hero by some people.

What You and Your Child Can Do

Stage Set. Read a story with your child, choosing one that has an especially strong setting. At the end of the story, get out a big sheet of white paper with which you can explore the setting you just read about. If your child just finished *Beauty and the Beast,* for example, have her draw the Beast's castle. Put in all the rooms, staircases, kitchens, and so on. Add rugs, pictures, and furnishings.

Who's Who. After you finish reading a story with your child, or after your child finishes a book, have her draw a picture of her favorite character. Use the clues found in the book: What does the character look like? What does the character wear?

Diorama. It's important to have your second grader begin to pay attention to the descriptions of the settings that appear in the books she reads. Choose a book to read together and pay special attention to the clues the author gives about setting—place, time of year, and location. Get a cardboard box and create that setting to make it look as much like the setting in the book as possible. Use paints, markers, material, glue, buttons, glitter—anything you can think of to make the diorama come alive.

What Tests May Ask

Standardized tests at this age will assess your child's understanding of a character by presenting a passage and then asking her to answer questions about the character and the character's motivation. Your child should read the passage closely, looking for clues to figure out how the character feels and what the person is like. Likewise, questions about setting that appear in given passages can help determine if your child is also paying attention to these important written clues.

Practice Skill: Characters and Settings

Directions: Read the passage. Choose the best answer to each question.

The New Boy

Jose walked slowly into the crowded cafeteria. Kids were sitting side by side on all the tables, laughing and talking to each other. No one looked his way. His tray felt heavier and heavier in his hands as he walked into the room.

How he missed Jim and Sandy from his old school! They always had a favorite table by the door, where they could jump up and get extra ice cream if there was time. Here, the table by the door was filled with giggling girls.

"Jose!" he heard someone call. "Hey, Jose!" Jose turned his head and saw a freckled boy smiling. "Come on over and sit with us!" the boy called, motioning to him.

Example:

Why is Jose nervous?

- Ⓐ He's worried about a test.
- Ⓑ He is new at school.
- Ⓒ He's performing in a play.
- Ⓓ He forgot his lunch money.

Answer:

- Ⓑ He is new at school.

13 How does Jose feel?

- Ⓐ He is excited about being in a new school.
- Ⓑ He is angry about leaving the old school.
- Ⓒ He is tired from carrying his tray.
- Ⓓ He is anxious about being the new boy.

14 Where does this story take place?

- Ⓐ in the auditorium
- Ⓑ in a classroom
- Ⓒ in the cafeteria
- Ⓓ in the gym

15 What is the location of this story like?

- Ⓐ silent and empty
- Ⓑ noisy and crowded
- Ⓒ dark and scary
- Ⓓ bright and hot

16 How does Jose probably feel when the freckled boy calls to him?

- Ⓐ angry
- Ⓑ happy
- Ⓒ lonesome
- Ⓓ mad

(See page 134 for the answer key.)

CHAPTER 11

Reading Comprehension

Second grade is the time when most elementary schools (and standardized tests) begin to put a heavy emphasis on reading comprehension—that is, understanding what has been read. As second graders get better at recognizing words, they also get much better at understanding stories in general. No longer do children this age have to struggle along, pausing to puzzle out every few words they encounter.

Still, teaching reading comprehension is not easy. It's all about thinking, which is harder to teach than simply how to say the letter m or the sum of $1 + 1$.

Reading comprehension really involves putting together a whole series of skills, including summarizing, predicting, sequencing, and drawing conclusions—higher-level skills that are only beginning to develop in second grade.

What Second Graders Should Know

While first graders struggle to simply identify individual words, most second graders have gone far beyond this to be able to assimilate the entire meaning from the sentences and paragraphs they read. During this year, most will begin to critically evaluate what they read.

At this age, second graders are just starting to be able to predict what will happen in a story. They can understand cause and effect, and they can draw conclusions based on the information they have read. If the author presents a number of facts to support the notion that walking is exercise and exercise is good, many second graders will draw the conclusion that walking can be a beneficial form of exercise.

These far more sophisticated readers can also pick out the implied feelings and motivations of characters they read, allowing them to compare and contrast one story or idea with another. Because their understanding of the stories they read is far more complete, they can now come up with a a an accurate title for a paragraph or brief story, which indicates their new ability to pick out the key points in writing.

What You and Your Child Can Do

Read. It's not too late to start if you've not been reading routinely to your child—and you should continue if you have been reading out loud for some time. Reading out loud helps your child get used to following the thread of a story and understanding the events as he hears them. Continue reading to him and let him read to you.

Read Magazines. Subscribe to age-appropriate magazines such as *Stone Soup, American Girl,* or *National Geographic Junior.*

Just the Facts, Ma'am. Encourage your child to read a variety of newspapers—and give him the "who what where when" quiz. Point out short articles in the newspaper or your magazines that you think would interest him. If he has trouble reading the articles, help him. After he's finished, get a notebook and ask him the "who what where when" of the article. See how many he can name!

Play Other Eyes. This activity is a good way to get your child to think about how the story might change if it were told from another perspective. This activity works very well for tales with a strong moral, such as the *Three Billy Goats Gruff.* After you finish reading the story with your child, ask him how the story might be different if told not from the goats' perspective but from the troll underneath the bridge. Or in the *Little House* books, how might the story be altered if it were told by a Native American child watching Laura Ingalls and her family build a log cabin on land where the Native American once roamed?

Help Your Child. You can boost your child's comprehension by encouraging him to make predictions as he reads; compare and contrast stories, characters, and settings; talk about causes and effects; infer meaning; and expand his vocabulary.

Jump Ahead. If your child reads ahead in the book you're reading to him at night, don't scold! Just ask him to summarize the chapters you've missed, and keep going.

Predicting Outcomes

Being able to predict the outcome of a story will help improve a child's reading comprehension. To be a good reader, he will have to become a good guesser—what might the next word be, what might the character do, how might the story end?

What Second Graders Should Know

You'd be surprised how hard it can be for a second grader to predict things, especially since so many youngsters this age are concerned about not making mistakes. After all, to be able to predict is to be willing to take a risk, and chil-dren this age are notoriously reluctant risk takers.

What You and Your Child Can Do

Predict! Get your child into the habit of predicting events by asking him to predict events around him—not just things in books. When you go out to eat, ask him to predict what Dad is going to order. What will Aunt Louise give him for his birthday? While you're waiting in the doctor's office, ask him to predict what the man across the room does for a living. Are there any clues in his clothes or attitude?

Practice. You can help your child learn to take risks by doing lots of predicting. When you choose a book together, ask: Are you going to like this book? As you begin to read, ask him what he thinks the book is about. What does he think might happen next?

Play Magazine ESP. When you're in a bookstore, stop by the magazine section with your child. Look at the titles and ask him what he thinks the stories might be about. (Choose magazines that are of interest to him, either about his hobbies or magazines designed for kids.)

What Tests May Ask

Standardized tests for second graders will assess their ability to predict the outcome by presenting a passage and asking: What do you think will happen next? What do you think will happen in the end? Tests also may present a title and ask second graders to predict what the story might be about.

Practice Skill: Predicting Outcomes

Directions: Read the passage. Choose the best answer for each question.

Example:

What is the best title for this passage?

The first settlers from England arrived in Virginia on December 4, 1619. The day they got to the new world was to be a day of giving thanks. They shared their blessings and looked forward to the new year. In 1621 the governor of Massachusetts set aside a special day for giving thanks.

- Ⓐ How Thanksgiving Started
- Ⓑ What Do You Eat on Thanksgiving?
- Ⓒ Pilgrims and Indians
- Ⓓ November Holidays

Answer:

- Ⓐ How Thanksgiving Started

Story

Moths and butterflies belong to the same insect family. They are often hard to tell apart, but they are different. Most moths fly at night. Most butterflies like the daytime. Moths are usually not as brightly colored as butterflies. When a moth is resting, it folds its wings. Butterflies like to spread out their wings.

1 What is the best title for this passage?

- Ⓐ What Are Moths?
- Ⓑ How Are Moths and Butterflies Different?
- Ⓒ I Like Insects
- Ⓓ Moths and Butterflies Are Bad

2 What is a book titled *Sue and June Go to the Beach,* most likely to be about?

- Ⓐ a tall tale about two rabbits
- Ⓑ a mystery involving secrets in a clock
- Ⓒ two friends who take a seashore vacation
- Ⓓ a sad story about a family who loses everything in a fire

3 The best title for a book about the life of a boy named Tom Sawyer is

- Ⓐ The Adventures of Tom Sawyer.
- Ⓑ Tom and Me.
- Ⓒ Wynken, Blynken and Nod.
- Ⓓ The Encyclopedia of Sea Creatures.

Directions: Read the following passage and then choose the sentence describing what would logically happen next.

Jim hooked a lead rope to the horse's halter. He led the horse out of the barn and tied him to a fence. First, Jim placed a blanket on the horse's back. Next, he put a saddle on the horse's back and tightened the girth.

4 Ⓐ Jim lay down and went to sleep.

Ⓑ The horse ate some hay in his stall.

Ⓒ The sun went behind a cloud.

Ⓓ Jim mounted the horse and rode away.

Directions: Read the following passages. Choose the statement that best describes what each story will probably be about.

It was a dark and stormy night. The trees crashed against the old house, and a shutter creaked mournfully on its squeaky hinges.

5 Ⓐ The story will probably be a scary mystery.

Ⓑ The story will probably be very funny.

Ⓒ The story will probably be about happy farm animals.

Ⓓ The story will probably be about science facts.

During the California gold rush in the 1850s, a clothes maker named Levi Strauss noticed that miners often ruined their clothes as they worked the mines. He started making sturdier pants out of thick canvas. They sold well.

6 Ⓐ This story will probably be a scary mystery.

Ⓑ This story will probably be a factual article about clothes.

Ⓒ This story will probably make people laugh.

Ⓓ This story will probably be about a happy family in Boston.

(See page 134 for the answer key.)

Drawing Conclusions

A *conclusion* is a sort of judgment that a person makes as a result of certain clues. If your child walks into his classroom and everyone there is wearing party hats and waving blowers, he can conclude that there's a birthday party going on. In reading, your child will be expected to gather the clues planted by the author and draw conclusions as a result of those clues.

What Second Graders Should Know

While younger children are unable to appreciate the deeper meanings embedded in many stories, second graders can appreciate these more complex and sometimes hidden morals. For example, a child in second grade who reads *Beauty and the Beast* will understand the moral—that it's important not to judge someone by how he looks. By middle to late second grade, he is probably becoming a more sophisticated reader in yet another sense: He can now understand and infer subtle emotional clues. If your child can read between the lines, that means he is making inferences—a skill that many second graders begin to develop this year.

The ability to understand a character's feelings involves not only the ability to understand the words presented but also to draw inferences from sometimes-subtle wording and implied action. Most early second graders will struggle with identifying feelings other than those that are blatantly presented. For example, unless the author specifically says, "Joe was sad," many early second graders won't be able to understand the feelings reflected in a sentence such as this: "As Joe's mother welcomed his cousin Sue, Joe sighed and walked out of the room." As second grade continues, however, more and more readers will develop depth and perception as they read.

What You and Your Child Can Do

You can help your child learn how to reach conclusions and make inferences by gently guiding him to gather clues and then sum up what he's learned. For example, let's say your child reads a book about kittens in which he learns that mother cats take care of their babies by making a nest in a safe place, bringing them food, teaching them to hunt, and carrying them in her mouth one by one to a new nest if there is danger. You can then ask him what conclusions he can make about mother cats. You're looking for an answer along these lines: They are loving mothers who take good care of their babies.

Ask Questions. As you finish a story with your child, ask him questions that require him to read between the lines. If you're reading *The Wind in the Willows* and Mole seems reluctant to get into Ratty's boat, ask your child if he thinks that Mole likes boats. The author may not have come right out and said so in that chapter, but by hearing about Mole's reluctance, your child should be able to figure out that Mole may be afraid of the water and boats.

Play Conclusion Caper. Here's a good game for a wet weekend when your child has nothing to do. Get a set of index cards and write a series of clues, one to a card. Hide them around the house for your child to find. Once he finds them all (tell him how many you've hidden so it's not too hard), have him read the clues in order and then come to a conclusion.

Sample clues:

1. At the store I got my grocery cart.
2. I bought gingerbread mix, flour, icing, sprinkles, peppermint sticks, and chocolate wafers.

3. I went to the dairy case.
4. I got butter, milk, and eggs.
5. I went to the department store.
6. I bought a set of special molds.
7. I went back home.
8. We're going to have lots of fun today in the kitchen!

Conclusion: We're making a gingerbread house!

What Tests May Ask

Standardized tests will assess how well your child can make conclusions and draw inferences from written material by presenting a story and asking questions about that passage.

Your child should read the entire passage first, looking for clues to help answer the questions. Once he draws a conclusion about what he's read, he should look for at least two details in the passage to support the answer.

Practice Skill: Drawing Conclusions

Directions: Read the passage. Choose the best answer to each question.

The Snake

Kara and her friend Kate were sailing down the stream. As they neared the shore, Kate suddenly pointed to the sand.

"Look!" she cried. A long, black snake was turning to look at them.

Kara leaned over and gently poked the snake with her paddle. With a warning hiss, the snake's head flashed forward. He bit the paddle!

"Do you think he's poisonous?" Kate asked nervously as Kara grabbed back the paddle.

"I don't know, but let's get out of here! I don't want to find out!" Kara said.

Example:

You can tell from the story that Kara and Kate are in a

Ⓐ car.

Ⓑ boat.

Ⓒ hot air balloon.

Ⓓ train.

Answer:

Ⓑ boat.

---

7 What will probably happen next?

Ⓐ The snake will bite Kate.

Ⓑ Kara will fall out of the boat.

Ⓒ Kate and Kara will capture the snake.

Ⓓ Kate and Kara will paddle away.

---

8 Who is Kara?

Ⓐ Kate's aunt

Ⓑ Kate's mother

Ⓒ the snake

Ⓓ Kate's friend

---

9 Why did Kate and Kara decide to leave?

Ⓐ They were hungry.

Ⓑ It was getting late.

Ⓒ They were sleepy.

Ⓓ They were afraid of the snake.

---

10 Read the passage and answer the question.

Mom thanked Johnny for doing the dishes for her while she was at work. "But I didn't do them!" Johnny said, surprised. "Maybe Tara did them." Johnny's brother Steve grinned to himself from the sofa and thought, "I surprised Mom!"

Who did the dishes for Mom?

Ⓐ Johnny

Ⓑ Mom

Ⓒ Steve

Ⓓ Tara

(See page 134 for the answer key.)

Cause and Effect

Cause and effect simply means something happens that leads to something else. In Cynthia Rylant's *The Bookshop Dog,* the main character goes into the hospital so someone else comes to take care of her dog. The cause: a hospital visit. The effect: someone else had to take care of the bookshop dog.

What Second Graders Should Know

In second grade, children are learning that for every cause there is an effect. If they don't brush their teeth, they will get cavities. If they don't do their homework, their teacher will be displeased. At the same time, they are learning that books have causes and effects, too. Something happens in a story, and something else occurs as a result.

What You and Your Child Can Do

Make Your Own Machine. Explain to your child about the fanciful designs of inventor

Rube Goldberg, who designed incredible machines to perform simple tasks. Then sit down with him to design his own machine. Decide what you'd like to accomplish (pour orange juice in the morning, for example), and then start off with a drawing of one piece of the machine to do that. See what you can come up with.

Make a Game. This is a terrific activity your second grader will love that also helps teach the idea of cause and effect. To make your own game board, take an old game board and cover it with wrapping paper, design side down. (Most wrapping paper is plain white on the inside). If your child's favorite book is *Uncle Wiggly,* have him draw Uncle Wiggly's house at the top corner of the board, and Uncle Wiggly at the bottom opposite corner. Now connect the two with a winding path of circles. In every other circle, write things like "Meet Nurse Jane Fuzzy Wuzzy: Go ahead two" or "Meet a bad wolf: Go back two." As you play the game, read the messages out loud. Explain which is the cause, and which is the effect: "Oh, look. I met Nurse Jane. I get to go ahead two." The first player to reach Uncle Wiggly's house wins.

Before That! Take opportunities in everyday life to point out cause and effect by asking your child to imagine what happened just before—if you see a cat racing across the street, ask your child to image what happened right before this to set the cat off. If you see a man fixing a flat tire by the side of the road, ask your child what might have happened right before to cause the flat tire.

Silly Science. Science is all about cause and effect. You could buy a "slime science" or other silly science kit to play with your child—or try your own experiments around the house. Try making a baking powder volcano: Have your child shape clay into a volcano shape, with a crater at the top. Drop in some baking powder (add food coloring if you want), and then drizzle on vinegar. Watch the lava flow!

What Tests May Ask

Standardized tests for the second grade usually assess cause and effect by presenting a passage and then asking questions about the passage. To answer the questions, the reader must understand what is going on in the story and be able to infer what caused something to happen. Students should look for clue words such as *because, so, since* or *as a result* that indicate cause and effect.

Practice Skill: Cause and Effect

Directions: Read this passage and then answer the question.

Tim always picked on the other children in his class. No one wanted to play with him. What the others did not know was that at home, Tim's older brother Bob always picked on Tim. So did all of Bob's friends.

Example:

Why did Bob's friends pick on Tim?

Ⓐ because Bob did

Ⓑ because they didn't have brothers

Ⓒ because Tim was a brat

Ⓓ because they didn't have fathers

Answer:

Ⓐ because Bob did

11 Why do you think Tim picked on the other boys and girls?

   Ⓐ Others always picked on him.

   Ⓑ He was bad.

   Ⓒ He was a boy.

   Ⓓ He spoke Spanish.

Christopher Columbus was a brilliant sea captain. In 1492 he sailed three ships from Spain westward. He hoped to reach China and Japan. Instead, he landed on San Salvador in the Bahamas. As a result, his discovery brought Europeans to America.

12 Christopher Columbus was

   Ⓐ a young man.

   Ⓑ a brilliant sea captain.

   Ⓒ running away to sea.

   Ⓓ friends with the king of Spain.

---

13 When Columbus left Spain, he was hoping to

   Ⓐ go on a long vacation.

   Ⓑ catch a lot of fish.

   Ⓒ discover England.

   Ⓓ discover a new route to China and Japan.

---

14 As a result of Columbus' voyage,

   Ⓐ Europeans came to America.

   Ⓑ slave trade was established.

   Ⓒ new kinds of food were discovered.

   Ⓓ gold was discovered.

(See page 134 for the answer key.)

CHAPTER 12

Literary Genres

Once a child has mastered the basics of reading words and sentences, a whole new world opens up: literature. By second grade, a wide variety of different genres (types) of literature are introduced, ranging from poetry to biography, tall tales, fantasy, fact, and fiction.

Very young readers accept what they read literally: If it's written down, it must be true. (In the 1950s, many first graders believed that Dick, Jane, Sally, their dog Spot, and their cat Puff really existed.) But by second grade, many children have become more realistic.

They recognize that dinosaurs no longer roam the earth and that science fiction is just that—fiction. By this age, your child is beginning to discern reality from fantasy in what she sees on television, in the stories you read to her, and in what she herself reads.

By second grade, most children are beginning to understand the difference between fact and opinion. Most second graders still struggle with subtle distinctions between the two, but they should be able to discriminate fact from opinion in blatant examples.

Over time they can give examples of poetry, memoirs, letters, songs, brochures, and other specific kinds of writing. They discuss what they see in these forms and can show their grasp of them by reproducing them in their own writing. They can see a bigger idea or theme at work and collect evidence of that theme.

By the end of the second grade, most students can write in a variety of styles, including stories, poems, songs, and plays, conforming to the appropriate form.

Fact versus Opinion

Facts are simply bits of information that are true, such as the gross national product of Ethiopia or the amount of rain you can expect in Florida in the summer. An *opinion* is something quite different: It's a statement of what someone thinks or believes about something, such as Ethiopia's financial picture or Florida's climate.

Fact: It's raining today.

Opinion: I think this is the crummiest weather we've ever had!

What Second Graders Should Know

There is a big difference between a fact and an opinion, and by second grade your child will begin to see this difference.

What You and Your Child Can Do

Fact-Opinion Survey. Take a sheet of paper and a newspaper and tell your child you're having a "fact-opinion hunt." Divide the paper into two columns, one labeled "facts" and one labeled "opinions." Open the paper to the advertisement section, and have your child write down "facts" or "opinions" under the appropriate column. Set a timer for two or three minutes. If there is more than one child, stage a competition. Once the bell rings, discuss the facts and opinions and the difference between them.

Critic for a Day. To help your child see the difference between fact and opinion, appoint her the "family critic"—have her vote thumbs up or down on various TV shows, movies, video games, or movies for the family. Have her describe the show (the facts) and then give a rating (her opinion). Point out the difference.

What Tests May Ask

Standardized tests for second grade will assess whether your child can tell the difference between fact and opinion. Your child will be expected to read a passage and then answer questions about whether each idea in the passage is a fact or an opinion.

To decide which is which, your child should look for something that can be proven true—that's a fact. Something that is a feeling or a belief is an opinion.

Practice Skill: Fact versus Opinion

Directions: Read the passage. Choose the best answer to each question.

Sharpies Are Best

Corky Smith is the best scooter-rider in the county. She practices long hours every day. And her scooter of choice? A Sharpie!

"I love my Sharpie!" she says proudly. "I wouldn't use any other scooter."

Sharpies are the king of scooters. They are the fastest, smoothest-riding scooters available today. You can tell it's a Sharpie by the neon-green wheels and the giant S on the handlebars. Nobody beats a Sharpie! It's the best scooter around. Get yours today if you want to be the best!

Example:

What is a Sharpie?

Ⓐ a bike

Ⓑ a scooter

Ⓒ a car

Ⓓ a skateboard

Answer:

Ⓑ a scooter

1 Which idea from the passage is a fact?

Ⓐ nobody beats a Sharpie.

Ⓑ Sharpies are the king of scooters.

Ⓒ a Sharpie is a brand of scooter.

Ⓓ Sharpies are wonderful.

2 Which idea from this passage is an opinion?

Ⓐ Corky rides a Sharpie.

Ⓑ A Sharpie is a scooter.

Ⓒ Corky practices long hours.

Ⓓ Nobody beats a Sharpie.

3 The author's purpose in this passage is to

Ⓐ explore Corky's riding ability.

Ⓑ explain how scooters are ridden.

Ⓒ convince you to buy a Sharpie.

Ⓓ explain how scooters are made.

Directions: Choose which of these sentences tells the writer's **opinion.**

The Miller Company is run by good people. They make ice cream. The company is in Vermont. The company pays workers bonuses when they work hard. They are the best!

4 Ⓐ The Miller Company makes ice cream.

   Ⓑ The company is run by good people.

   Ⓒ The company is in Vermont.

   Ⓓ They pay their workers bonuses when they work hard.

(See page 134 for the answer key.)

Reality versus Fantasy

What is real and what is fantasy? The difference between what is real and what is only imagined is an important one in literature, and in second grade students are introduced to both genres.

What Second Graders Should Know

Second graders are usually introduced to a wide range of classic fantasy stories and are taught to compare these rich forms of literature with reality-based stories.

What You and Your Child Can Do

Reality Check. As you read a child's fantasy book (such as Madeleine L'Engle's *A Wrinkle in Time*), discuss with your child the difference between reality and fantasy. Get a notebook, and on one side of the page, write "reality" and on the other, "fantasy." After reading a chapter in *Wrinkle,* take turns writing sentences about what could really happen under "reality" and what couldn't happen under "fantasy":

Reality	Fantasy
Meg gets scared of the storm.	There is such a thing as a tesseract.
Charles Wallace makes hot chocolate.	Meg travels through time to another planet.

What Tests May Ask

Standardized tests in second grade usually assess a child's understanding of the difference between reality and fantasy by presenting a passage and asking a child to discern which statements are true and which are grounded in fantasy.

Practice Skill: Reality versus Fantasy

Directions: Choose the correct answer for each of the following questions.

5 Which of these sentences is true?

   Ⓐ Humans have walked on the moon.

   Ⓑ Humans have walked on the sun.

   Ⓒ Humans live on Mars.

   Ⓓ Pirates still roam the seas.

6 Which of these sentences is based on fantasy?

   Ⓐ Spaceships can fly through the air.

   Ⓑ Dinosaurs once roamed the earth.

   Ⓒ Unicorns are still alive on this planet.

   Ⓓ Giant telescopes can peer far into space.

(See page 134 for the answer key.)

Biography

A wide variety of biographies are introduced in the second year involving past and present leaders and heroes in the movies and sports and the fields of science, medicine, and government. No matter what interests your child may have, it should be possible to find a biography that she will be able to relate to.

What Second Graders Should Know

By the end of second grade, your child should understand what a biography is—a story about a person—and what kinds of information would be expected to be included in a biography. She should have read in class several biographies of different types of people at different times in history.

What You and Your Child Can Do

The Tonight Show. After you read a biography with your child, have her take "the mike" and sit down for an interview. Have your child pretend she is the character in the book you've just read, and ask her all kinds of questions. See how well she can put herself into the character's shoes.

Writing Her Life Story. What better way to learn all about a biography than to write her own? Get your child some sheets of paper, colored pens, photographs, and stickers, and have her write her own biography. Make sure she includes all of the most important points that have occurred so far in her life. (Making a brief outline of her life might help her organize her thoughts.) Include a construction paper cover, and staple the sheets together.

Minibiography. After your child finishes a favorite book, have her write a biography of one of the characters in the book. If she loves the book *Leah's Pony*, have her write a biography about a minor character—perhaps the pony himself. If it's the *Little House* series of books, have her write a biography of Laura's older sister, Mary.

What Tests May Ask

In assessing children's understanding of biographies, standardized tests during the second grade will present a brief biographical sketch and then ask children a series of questions about the passage. These questions may ask children to determine what genre the passage is and ask specific questions about the person in the biography.

Practice Skill: Biography

Directions: Read the following passage. Choose the correct answer to each question.

Guion "Guy" Bluford, Jr., was born in Philadelphia, Pennsylvania, in 1942. He was the first African-American to travel into space. The flight began on Aug. 30, 1983. His job was mission specialist, which meant that he was responsible for the equipment and controls on that flight. This was also the first mission to take off and land at night. After graduating from Penn State University, he served as a pilot in the U.S. Air Force.

7 Guy Bluford, Jr., was

Ⓐ the first African-American in space.

Ⓑ the youngest person in space.

Ⓒ the first teacher to go into space.

Ⓓ the first African-American to walk in space.

8 Bluford was responsible for

(A) meals in space.

(B) exercise in space.

(C) everyone's health in space.

(D) equipment and controls on the spacecraft.

Cleopatra was born in 69 B.C. and died in 30 B.C. Little is known about her childhood. She became queen of Egypt at age 17. Although she died young (at age 39), she is remembered as one of the most important women in history because of her friendships with Julius Caesar and Marc Antony.

9 Cleopatra is remembered as

(A) a good doctor.

(B) a great queen of Egypt.

(C) an old warrior.

(D) a good cook.

(See page 134 for the answer key.)

Poetry

Many second graders love poetry, and they are introduced to this form of literature in their classes. Poetry can teach particularly colorful language as well as more traditional values such as honesty, courage, and caring.

What Second Graders Should Know

Your child should have a basic understanding of a poem, the rhythmic effects of certain sounds and repetitions, and the use of words to help form mental pictures.

What You and Your Child Can Do

Write a Poem. Many second graders love poems because with poetry, they can express themselves without needing to worry about punctuation, complete sentences, and all those grammatical "shoulds." Take time to sit down with your child and try to paint a picture in a poem.

Read Aloud. Poems often sound best when read aloud. Read often to your second grader, and pick up a poetry book now and then. Shel Silverstein's funny verses are big favorites of this age. After you read a poem, ask your child what she likes about the poem, what the poem makes her feel or think of. Ask your child if there is a sound she notices in a particular poem. How does the poet use sound to make the poem more effective?

What Tests May Ask

Standardized tests in second grade assess a child's understanding of poetry by presenting a poem or part of a poem, and then asking specific questions about the poem. Questions may include items asking about the poet's intentions, specific topics within the poem, the title, and why the poem was written.

Practice Skill: Poetry

Directions: Read the poem. Answer the following questions about the poem.

The Moon

By Robert Louis Stevenson

The moon has a face like the clock in the hall;

She shines on thieves climbing garden wall,

On streets and fields and harbor bays,
And birdies asleep in the forks of
trees.

Squallering cat and the squeaking
mouse,

The howling dog by the door of the
house,

The bat that lies in bed at noon,
All love to be out by the light of the
moon.

But all of the things that belong to
the day

Cuddle in sleep to stay out of her way;
And flowers and children close their
eyes

Until in the morning the sun will
arise.

10 What does the author mean by
the word <u>squallering</u>?

   Ⓐ sleeping

   Ⓑ walking

   Ⓒ meowing loudly

   Ⓓ giggling

11 From this poem, you can tell that

   Ⓐ the moon lights up lots of
things.

   Ⓑ it was a dark night.

   Ⓒ the author doesn't like to
sleep.

   Ⓓ it's Christmas time.

12 What does the title tell us about
the poem?

   Ⓐ Children like to sleep.

   Ⓑ Bats like to eat fruit.

   Ⓒ The moon is the main topic.

   Ⓓ There are a lot of robbers
around.

Paul Revere's Ride

By Henry Wadsworth Longfellow

Listen, my children, and you shall
hear

Of the midnight ride of Paul Revere,

On the eighteenth of April, in
Seventy-five;

Hardly a man is now alive

Who remembers that famous day and
year.

He said to his friend, "If the British
march

By land or sea from the town tonight,

Hang a lantern aloft in the belfry
arch

Of the North Church tower as a signal light—

One, if by land, and two, if by sea;

And I on the opposite shore will be

Ready to ride and spread the alarm

Through every Middlesex village and
farm,

For the country folk to be up and to
arm."

13 What does the author mean by "one, if by land"?

- Ⓐ There will be one knock on the door if the enemy is coming.
- Ⓑ One lantern will be hung if the enemy appears by land.
- Ⓒ One enemy is coming.
- Ⓓ One army is coming.

14 Who is the "he" in the phrase "He said to his friend"?

- Ⓐ George Washington
- Ⓑ a country man
- Ⓒ Paul Revere
- Ⓓ an unknown soldier

15 What happens next once the lanterns are hung in Old North Church?

- Ⓐ There is a party for Paul Revere in the church.
- Ⓑ There is a fire in Middlesex, and Paul Revere will put it out.
- Ⓒ There is a battle between Paul Revere and the British.
- Ⓓ Paul Revere rides to warn the villagers that the British are coming.

(See page 134 for the answer key.)

CHAPTER 13

Study Skills

Study skills are an important part of a second grader's life, and a solid understanding now will help provide a good foundation for the rest of your child's educational career. Study skills typically taught in the second grade include alphabetical order to the third letter, identifying words in a dictionary, graphs, and parts of a book.

What Second Graders Should Know

Study skills are vital to students for their entire school career, so you can expect your child's teacher to begin to introduce basic study skills during this year. By the end of second grade, your child should be able to alphabetize words to the third letter. He should understand the basics of a dictionary and be able to look up simple words. He should be able to read simple graphs and tables and recognize the basic parts of a book: title, table of contents, and index.

What You and Your Child Can Do

Personal Library. By now you've probably gotten the message that reading is crucial to success in developing good reading and writing skills. Setting up a corner of your child's room as his personal library is one way of showing him how important you think books are. Once you've gotten the shelves together, let him set up his books himself, arranging them by author alphabetically. This will provide a good bit of practice in alphabetization.

Make Your Own Dictionary. Encourage your child to make his own dictionary featuring his favorite words. Have him create a book page for each letter of the alphabet, writing the entry letter very large at the top of the page. Next, have him print his favorite words on each of the corresponding pages. Then encourage him to illustrate his dictionary with drawings or art that he has cut out of magazines. Once he's listed all his favorite words, have him try to come up with at least one word for each page of the book. Add new words as he comes across them. Punch holes in the pages, add two cardboard covers, and tie them together with bright yarn.

Alphabetical Order

Words are alphabetized according to their first letter:

apple

clothes

horse

If all the first letters are the same, your child should move to the second letter:

hat

heat

horse

If the first and second letters are the same, your child should move to the third letter:

home

horse

house

What Second Graders Should Know

Putting words into alphabetical order is a task for second graders. You should expect most children to be able to alphabetize words to the third letter by the end of second grade.

What You and Your Child Can Do

Monkey in the Middle. For this game, give your child two words. Have him come up with a word that would fit in between the two. Start out with words that begin with different letters; as he gets better, use words with the same first letters. Finally, move on to letters with the same first two letters.

List of Words. Give your child three lists of words—one set with different first letters, another set with the same first letters, and a third set with the same first two letters. Have him alphabetize them, and time him. See how long each list takes. If he enjoys this activity, work on improving his "personal best" time.

What Tests May Ask

Standardized tests in second grade will ask your child a series of questions about alphabetizing, assessing his skill to the third letter. Typically, the tests will present a list of words and ask your child to choose the word that will come next—or to choose the one word that does not fit.

Practice Skill: Alphabetical Order

Directions: In the following list of alphabetical words, choose the word that comes next in correct alphabetical order from the choices below.

Example:

can   dog   find

- Ⓐ apple
- Ⓑ boat
- Ⓒ cord
- Ⓓ goat

Answer:

- Ⓓ goat

---

1 apple   elephant   sun

- Ⓐ corn
- Ⓑ water
- Ⓒ dog
- Ⓓ run

---

2 bar   bean   bottle

- Ⓐ bear
- Ⓑ bun
- Ⓒ basket
- Ⓓ bore

---

3 baby   bad   basket

- Ⓐ bat
- Ⓑ bean
- Ⓒ bar
- Ⓓ bait

(See page 134 for the answer key.)

Dictionaries

If your child is to use a dictionary well, he must understand not only how to alphabetize words effectively but also how to use a dictionary's guide words. *Guide words* are those words at the top of a dictionary page that tell you the first and last word on each page. Using alphabetical order, if a word falls between these two guide words, it will be found on that page.

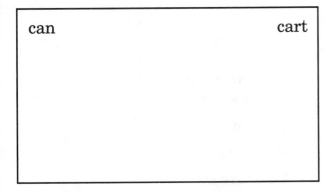

In the sample dictionary page above, the guide words *can* and *cart* indicate that you would find the word *candy* on that page because it falls alphabetically between the two guide words. You would not find *case* because that comes after the word *cart,* which is the last word on that page.

In addition to guide words, your child will learn about what to find in a typical dictionary entry—the definition, how to spell the word correctly, how to pronounce it, and how many syllables it has:

bay \bāy\ 1. an inlet of the sea or other body of water, usually smaller than a gulf.

From this entry, your child can learn what a bay is, that it has one syllable, and that the vowel says its name (has a long *a*).

What Second Graders Should Know

By second grade, your child should know what to find in a dictionary and how to find it. He should be able to use alphabetical skills and guide words to locate any word he needs to find.

What You and Your Child Can Do

Ready ... **Set** ... **Look It Up!** Get out your timer for this one. Write down a list of words of more than three letters. Give your child one word at a time, and set the timer to see how long it takes him to find the word. As his skill improves, use harder, more complex words. If you have more than one child, you can turn it into a competition and see who finds the word first. (Of course, you'll need two identical dictionaries for that one!)

Play Word Detective. Open a dictionary and cover up all the words on the page except for the two guide words. Ask your child to come up with a word that he thinks is on the page (that would fit alphabetically between the two guide words). Uncover the page and see if the word is there.

Model It. If you're reading and there's a word you don't understand, make sure your child sees you going to the dictionary to look it up. Ask your child what **he** thinks the word means. Involve him in the process.

Likewise, if he's reading and comes across a word he doesn't understand, don't just define it for him. Tell him to look it up, and follow through with him to make sure he does.

What Tests May Ask

Standardized tests for this age will assess how well your child understands what a dictionary entry means and how to look up words. Tests may present a sample dictionary page and ask your child to tell which word may—or may not—fall within two given guide words. Tests also may ask where you should look to find the answers to certain questions.

Practice Skill: Dictionary Entries

Directions: Read the following questions and choose the correct answer for each.

Example: Which word would you find on the following dictionary page, between the guide words *pat* and *pin*?

pat	pin

sat	send

Ⓐ put

Ⓑ par

Ⓒ pea

Ⓓ punt

Answer:

Ⓒ pea

4 What word would you find on the dictionary page above?

Ⓐ patty

Ⓑ pretty

Ⓒ putty

Ⓓ pot

5 Which word would you **not** find on the dictionary page above?

Ⓐ sew

Ⓑ pear

Ⓒ peony

Ⓓ paw

6 What word would you find on the dictionary page above?

Ⓐ sun

Ⓑ sent

Ⓒ surprise

Ⓓ Saturday

7 What word would you **not** find on the dictionary page above?

Ⓐ sunny

Ⓑ seat

Ⓒ saw

Ⓓ sea

8 If you wanted to find out how to pronounce the word *horror*, where would you look?

Ⓐ atlas

Ⓑ encyclopedia

Ⓒ dictionary

Ⓓ newspaper

9 What things could you **not** find in a dictionary?

Ⓐ how to pronounce a word

Ⓑ how many syllables a word has

Ⓒ how to spell a word

Ⓓ daily report of what is happening in the news

(See page 134 for the answer key.)

Graphs

Learning how to read charts and graphs is another important aspect of study skills that will be introduced in second grade. Bar graphs, line graphs, and picture graphs are typically discussed during this year.

What Second Graders Should Know

Although some schools introduce graphs in first grade, it is usually not until second grade that students are ready to understand the different types of graphs and interpret the information they can find there. They can both produce their own graphs and correctly gather information that others produce.

What You and Your Child Can Do

Graph It! Graphs can be a fun way of measuring and categorizing lots of things around the house. Get several sheets of paper and have your child design graphs to illustrate how many pairs of socks each member of the family has.

Be a Weatherperson. Get your child an inexpensive rain gauge, or make one from a plastic cup and a ruler. Have your child measure the rain for a week or a month, and graph the results. Temperature measurements and snow levels also work well.

What Tests May Ask

Standardized tests will present a variety of different types of graphs and ask specific questions based on the information that they contain. If your child has had lots of practice in interpreting graphs, these shouldn't be a surprise to him. Make sure he takes his time and studies the graphs carefully.

Practice Skill: Graphs

Directions: Look at the graph below. Choose the correct answer to each question.

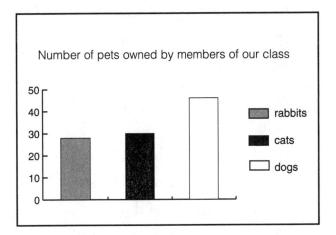

Example:

What does this graph represent?

Ⓐ the number of pets owned by members of our class

Ⓑ the number of students in the class

Ⓒ the number of horses owned by class

Ⓓ the number of students absent this week

Answer:

   (A) The number of pets owned by members of our class

---

10 What does the white bar represent?

   (A) the number of cats

   (B) the number of rabbits

   (C) the number of dogs

   (D) the number of students

---

11 What does the black bar represent?

   (A) the number of cats

   (B) the number of rabbits

   (C) the number of dogs

   (D) the number of students

---

12 What does the gray bar represent?

   (A) the number of cats

   (B) the number of rabbits

   (C) the number of dogs

   (D) the number of students

---

13 How many cats are owned by classmates?

   (A) about 30

   (B) about 10

   (C) about 45

   (D) none

(See page 134 for the answer key.)

Parts of a Book

Being able to understand the purpose of the various parts of a book is an important study skill that is introduced in the second grade. During this year, students become familiar with the title page, table of contents, bibliography, and index. It's also important that students know what sort of information they can find and how to locate it in each part of a book.

What Second Graders Should Know

Your second grader should have a solid understanding of the purpose of all the parts of a book. He should know that the title page contains the title of the book and the author's name, plus where and when the book was published. He should know that a table of contents tells him what information will be contained in the book and (usually) on what page the chapters begin. The bibliography reveals what other resources the author used to write the book, and the glossary is a sort of minidictionary that may explain some of the terms used in the book. Finally, the index is the place your child should go to find the exact page number for important terms or facts referred to in the book.

What You and Your Child Can Do

Make Your Own Book. One of the best ways to teach your child about the different parts of a book is to help him make his own, complete with table of contents and index. Have him number the pages so that it will be possible to create an index.

Play Wordfind. Teach your child how to use an index. Find a simple nonfiction book with a good index. Make a list of 10 terms that are listed in the index. Set the timer and call out the terms for him to locate in the book.

What Tests May Ask

Standardized tests will ask specific questions about the types of information that can be found in different parts of a book or where a child would go to find certain information.

Practice Skill: Parts of a Book

Directions: Choose the correct answer for the following questions.

Example:

Where would you look to find a definition of a word mentioned in a book on boats?

(A) glossary

(B) table of contents

(C) title page

(D) index

Answer:

(A) glossary

14 If Rachel wanted to find in a particular book the specific page that discussed Palomino ponies, where would she look?

(A) glossary

(B) table of contents

(C) title page

(D) index

15 As you read a book about stars, there is a word you don't understand. Where in the book would you find a definition of this word?

(A) table of contents

(B) glossary

(C) index

(D) title page

16 Sharon wants to get a general idea of the topics covered in her history book. She would look for that information in

(A) the table of contents.

(B) the glossary.

(C) the index.

(D) the title page.

(See page 134 for the answer key.)

Web Sites and Resources for More Information

Homework

Homework Central
http://www.HomeworkCentral.com
Terrific site for students, parents, and teachers, filled with information, projects, and more.

Win the Homework Wars
(Sylvan Learning Centers)
http://www.educate.com/online/qa_peters.html

Reading and Grammar Help

Born to Read: How to Raise a Reader
http://www.ala.org/alsc/raise_a_reader.html

Guide to Grammar and Writing
http://webster.commnet.edu/hp/pages/darling/grammar.htm
Help with "plague words and phrases," grammar FAQs, sentence parts, punctuation, rules for common usage.

Internet Public Library: Reading Zone
http://www.ipl.org/cgi-bin/youth/youth.out

Keeping Kids Reading and Writing
http://www.tiac.net/users/maryl/

U.S. Dept. of Education: Helping Your Child Learn to Read
http://www.ed.gov/pubs/parents/Reading/index.html

Math Help

Center for Advancement of Learning
http://www.muskingum.edu/%7Ecal/database/Math2.html
Substitution and memory strategies for math.

Center for Advancement of Learning
http://www.muskingum.edu/%7Ecal/database/Math1.html
General tips and suggestions.

Math.com
http://www.math.com
The world of math online.

Math.com
http://www.math.com/student/testprep.html
Get ready for standardized tests.

Math.com: Homework Help in Math
http://www.math.com/students/homework.html

Math.com: Math for Homeschoolers
http://www.math.com/parents/homeschool.html

The Math Forum: Problems and Puzzles
http://forum.swarthmore.edu/library/resource_types/problems_puzzles
Lots of fun math puzzles and problems for grades K through 12.

The Math Forum: Math Tips and Tricks
http://forum.swarthmore.edu/k12/mathtips/mathtips.html

Tips on Testing

Books on Test Preparation
http://www.testbooksonline.com/preHS.asp
This site provides printed resources for parents who wish to help their children prepare for standardized school tests.

Core Knowledge Web Site
http://www.coreknowledge.org/
Site dedicated to providing resources for parents; based on the books of E. D. Hirsch, Jr., who wrote the *What Your X Grader Needs to Know* series.

Family Education Network
http://www.familyeducation.com/article/0,1120,1-6219,00.html
This report presents some of the arguments against current standardized testing practices in the public schools. The site also provides links to family activities that help kids learn.

Math.com
http://www.math.com/students/testprep.html
Get ready for standardized tests.

Standardized Tests
http://arc.missouri.edu/k12/
K through 12 assessment tools and know-how.

Parents: Testing in Schools

KidSource: Talking to Your Child's Teacher about Standardized Tests
http://www.kidsource.com/kidsource/content2/talking.assessment.k12.4.html
This site provides basic information to help parents understand their children's test results and provides pointers for how to discuss the results with their children's teachers.

eSCORE.com: State Test and Education Standards
http://www.eSCORE.com
Find out if your child meets the necessary requirements for your local schools. A Web site with experts from Brazelton Institute and Harvard's Project Zero.

Overview of States' Assessment Programs
http://ericae.net/faqs/

Parent Soup
Education Central: Standardized Tests
http://www.parentsoup.com/edcentral/testing
A parent's guide to standardized testing in the schools, written from a parent advocacy standpoint.

National Center for Fair and Open Testing, Inc. (FairTest)
342 Broadway
Cambridge, MA 02139
(617) 864-4810
http://www.fairtest.org

National Parent Information Network
http://npin.org

Publications for Parents from the U.S. Department of Education
http://www.ed.gov/pubs/parents/
An ever-changing list of information for parents available from the U.S. Department of Education.

State of the States Report
http://www.edweek.org/sreports/qc99/states/indicators/in-intro.htm
A report on testing and achievement in the 50 states.

Testing: General Information

Academic Center for Excellence
http://www.acekids.com

American Association for Higher Education Assessment
http://www.aahe.org/assessment/web.htm

American Educational Research Association (AERA)
http://aera.net
An excellent link to reports on American education, including reports on the controversy over standardized testing.

American Federation of Teachers
555 New Jersey Avenue, NW
Washington, D.C. 20011

Association of Test Publishers Member Products and Services
http://www.testpublishers.org/memserv.htm

Education Week on the Web
http://www.edweek.org

ERIC Clearinghouse on Assessment and Evaluation
1131 Shriver Lab
University of Maryland
College Park, MD 20742
http://ericae.net
A clearinghouse of information on assessment and education reform.

FairTest: The National Center for Fair and Open Testing
http://fairtest.org/facts/ntfact.htm
http://fairtest.org/
The National Center for Fair and Open Testing is an advocacy organization working to end the abuses, misuses, and flaws of standardized testing and to ensure that evaluation of students and workers is fair, open, and educationally sound. This site provides many links to fact sheets, opinion papers, and other sources of information about testing.

National Congress of Parents and Teachers
700 North Rush Street
Chicago, Illinois 60611

National Education Association
1201 16th Street, NW
Washington, DC 20036

National School Boards Association
http://www.nsba.org
A good source for information on all aspects of public education, including standardized testing.

Testing Our Children: A Report Card on State Assessment Systems
http://www.fairtest.org/states/survey.htm
Report of testing practices of the states, with graphical links to the states and a critique of fair testing practices in each state.

Trends in Statewide Student Assessment Programs: A Graphical Summary
http://www.ccsso.org/survey96.html
Results of annual survey of states' departments of public instruction regarding their testing practices.

U.S. Department of Education
http://www.ed.gov/

Web Links for Parents Who Want to Help Their Children Achieve
http://www.liveandlearn.com/learn.html
This page offers many Web links to free and for-sale information and materials for parents who want to help their children do well in school. Titles include such free offerings as the Online Colors Game and questionnaires to determine whether your child is ready for school.

What Should Parents Know about Standardized Testing in the Schools?
http://www.rusd.k12.ca.us/parents/standard.html
An online brochure about standardized testing in the schools, with advice regarding how to become an effective advocate for your child.

Test Publishers Online

ACT: Information for Life's Transitions
http://www.act.org

American Guidance Service, Inc.
http://www.agsnet.com

Ballard & Tighe Publishers
http://www.ballard-tighe.com

Consulting Psychologists Press
http://www.cpp-db.com

CTB McGraw-Hill
http://www.ctb.com

Educational Records Bureau
http://www.erbtest.org/index.html

Educational Testing Service
http://www.ets.org

General Educational Development (GED) Testing Service
http://www.acenet.edu/calec/ged/home.html

Harcourt Brace Educational Measurement
http://www.hbem.com

Piney Mountain Press—A Cyber-Center for Career and Applied Learning
http://www.pineymountain.com

ProEd Publishing
http://www.proedinc.com

Riverside Publishing Company
http://www.hmco.com/hmco/riverside

Stoelting Co.
http://www.stoeltingco.com

Sylvan Learning Systems, Inc.
http://www.educate.com

Touchstone Applied Science Associates, Inc. (TASA)
http://www.tasa.com

Tests Online

(*Note:* We don't endorse tests; some may not have technical documentation. Evaluate the quality of any testing program before making decisions based on its use.)

Edutest, Inc.
http://www.edutest.com
Edutest is an Internet-accessible testing service that offers criterion-referenced tests for elementary school students, based upon the standards for K through 12 learning and achievement in the states of Virginia, California, and Florida.

Virtual Knowledge
http://www.smarterkids.com
This commercial service, which enjoys a formal partnership with Sylvan Learning Centers, offers a line of skills assessments for preschool through grade 9 for use in the classroom or the home. For free online sample tests, see the Virtual Test Center.

Read More about It

Abbamont, Gary W. *Test Smart: Ready-to-Use Test-Taking Strategies and Activities for Grades 5–12*. Upper Saddle River, NJ: Prentice Hall Direct, 1997.

Cookson, Peter W., and Joshua Halberstam. *A Parent's Guide to Standardized Tests in School: How to Improve Your Child's Chances for Success*. New York: Learning Express, 1998.

Frank, Steven, and Stephen Frank. *Test-Taking Secrets: Study Better, Test Smarter, and Get Great Grades (The Backpack Study Series)*. Holbrook, MA: Adams Media Corporation, 1998.

Gilbert, Sara Dulaney. *How to Do Your Best on Tests: A Survival Guide*. New York: Beech Tree Books, 1998.

Gruber, Gary. *Dr. Gary Gruber's Essential Guide to Test-Taking for Kids, Grades 3–5*. New York: William Morrow & Co., 1986.

————. *Gary Gruber's Essential Guide to Test-Taking for Kids, Grades 6, 7, 8, 9*. New York: William Morrow & Co., 1997.

Leonhardt, Mary. *99 Ways to Get Kids to Love Reading and 100 Books They'll Love*. New York: Crown, 1997.

————. *Parents Who Love Reading, Kids Who Don't: How It Happens and What You Can Do about It*. New York: Crown, 1995.

McGrath, Barbara B. *The Baseball Counting Book*. Watertown, MA: Charlesbridge, 1999.

————. *More M&M's Brand Chocolate Candies Math*. Watertown, MA: Charlesbridge, 1998.

Mokros, Janice R. *Beyond Facts & Flashcards: Exploring Math with Your Kids*. Portsmouth, NH: Heinemann, 1996.

Romain, Trevor, and Elizabeth Verdick. *True or False?: Tests Stink!* Minneapolis: Free Spirit Publishing Co., 1999.

Schartz, Eugene M. *How to Double Your Child's Grades in School: Build Brilliance and Leadership into Your Child—from Kindergarten to College—in Just 5 Minutes a Day*. New York: Barnes & Noble, 1999.

Taylor, Kathe, and Sherry Walton. *Children at the Center: A Workshop Approach to Standardized Test Preparation, K–8*. Portsmouth, NH: Heinemann, 1998.

Tobia, Sheila. *Overcoming Math Anxiety*. New York: W. W. Norton & Company, Inc., 1995.

Tufariello, Ann Hunt. *Up Your Grades: Proven Strategies for Academic Success*. Lincolnwood, IL: VGM Career Horizons, 1996.

Vorderman, Carol. *How Math Works*. Pleasantville, NY: Reader's Digest Association, Inc., 1996.

Zahler, Kathy A. *50 Simple Things You Can Do to Raise a Child Who Loves to Read*. New York: IDG Books, 1997.

What Your Child's Test Scores Mean

Several weeks or months after your child has taken standardized tests, you will receive a report such as the TerraNova Home Report found in Figures 1 and 2. You will receive similar reports if your child has taken other tests. We briefly examine what information the reports include.

Look at the first page of the Home Report. Note that the chart provides labeled bars showing the child's performance. Each bar is labeled with the child's National Percentile for that skill area. When you know how to interpret them, national percentiles can be the most useful scores you encounter on reports such as this. Even when you are confronted with different tests that use different scale scores, you can always interpret percentiles the same way, regardless of the test. A percentile tells the percent of students who score at or below that level. A percentile of 25, for example, means that 25 percent of children taking the test scored at or below that score. (It also means that 75 percent of students scored above that score.) Note that the average is always at the 50th percentile.

On the right side of the graph on the first page of the report, the publisher has designated the ranges of scores that constitute average, above average, and below average. You can also use this slightly more precise key for interpreting percentiles:

PERCENTILE RANGE	LEVEL
2 and Below	Deficient
3–8	Borderline
9–23	Low Average
24–75	Average
76–97	High Average
98 and Up	Superior

The second page of the Home report provides a listing of the child's strengths and weaknesses, along with keys for mastery, partial mastery, and non-mastery of the skills. Scoring services determine these breakdowns based on the child's scores as compared with those from the national norm group.

Your child's teacher or guidance counselor will probably also receive a profile report similar to the TerraNova Individual Profile Report, shown in Figures 3 and 4. That report will be kept in your child's permanent record. The first aspect of this report to notice is that the scores are expressed both numerically and graphically.

First look at the score bands under National Percentile. Note that the scores are expressed as bands, with the actual score represented by a dot within each band. The reason we express the scores as bands is to provide an idea of the amount by which typical scores may vary for each student. That is, each band represents a

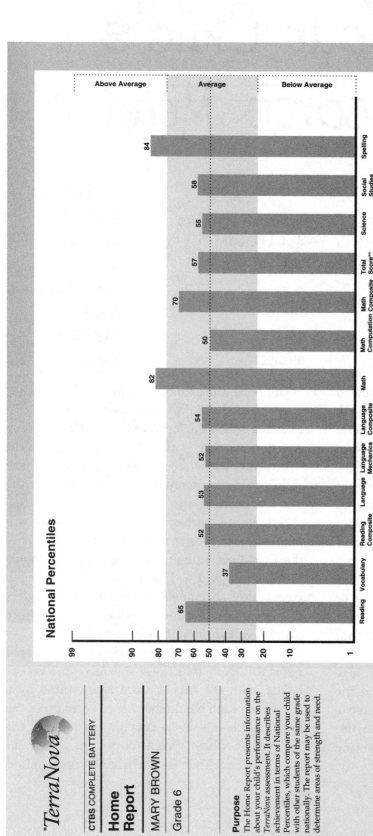

Figure 1 (SOURCE: CTB/McGraw-Hill, copyright © 1997. All rights reserved. Reproduced with permission.)

TerraNova

CTBS COMPLETE BATTERY

Home Report

MARY BROWN

Grade 6

Purpose

This page of the Home Report presents information about your child's strengths and needs. This information is provided to help you monitor your child's academic growth.

Simulated Data

Birthdate: 02/08/85
Special Codes:
A B C D E F G H I J K L M N O P Q R S T
3 5 9 7 3 2   1 1 1
Form/Level: A-16
Test Date: 11/01/99   Scoring: PATTERN (IRT)
QM: 08   Norms Date: 1996

Class: PARKER
School: WINFIELD
District: WINFIELD

City/State: WINFIELD, CA

CTB
McGraw-Hill

Page 2

CTBID:92123B821460001-04-00052-000054
W1 CB HR P2 Final:11/05

Strengths

Reading
● Basic Understanding
● Analyze Text

Vocabulary
● Word Meaning
● Words in Context

Language
● Editing Skills
● Sentence Structure

Language Mechanics
● Sentences, Phrases, Clauses

Mathematics
● Computation and Numerical Estimation
● Operation Concepts

Mathematics Computation
● Add Whole Numbers
● Multiply Whole Numbers

Science
● Life Science
● Inquiry Skills

Social Studies
● Geographic Perspectives
● Economic Perspectives

Spelling
● Vowels
● Consonants

Key ● Mastery

Needs

Reading
◐ Evaluate and Extend Meaning
○ Identify Reading Strategies

Vocabulary
○ Multimeaning Words

Language
◐ Writing Strategies

Language Mechanics
○ Writing Conventions

Mathematics
◐ Measurement
◐ Geometry and Spatial Sense

Mathematics Computation
○ Percents

Science
○ Earth and Space Science

Social Studies
◐ Historical and Cultural Perspectives

Spelling
No area of needs were identified for this content area

Key ◐ Partial Mastery   ○ Non-Mastery

General Interpretation

The left column shows your child's best areas of performance. In each case, your child has reached mastery level. The column at the right shows the areas within each test section where your child's scores are the lowest. In these cases, your child has not reached mastery level, although he or she may have reached partial mastery.

Figure 2 (SOURCE: CTB/McGraw-Hill, copyright © 1997. All rights reserved. Reproduced with permission.)

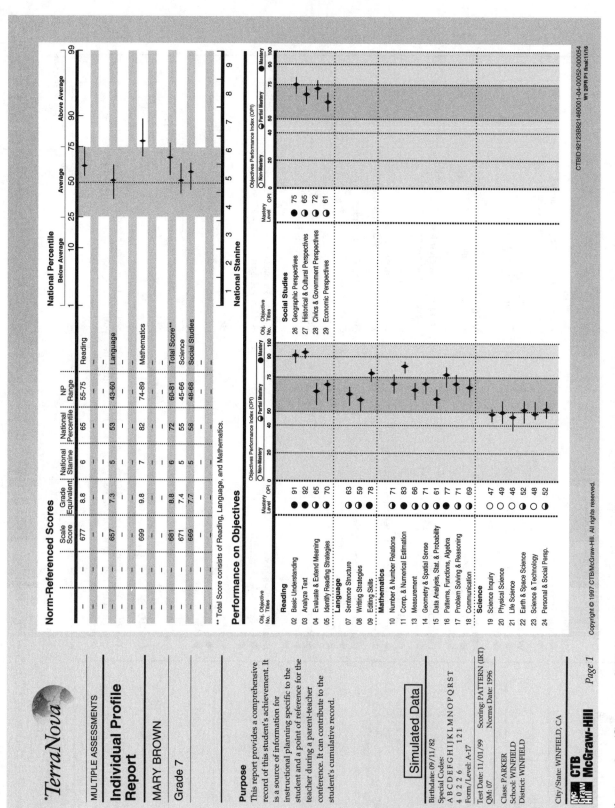

Figure 3 (SOURCE: CTB/McGraw-Hill, copyright © 1997. All rights reserved. Reproduced with permission.)

Observations

Norm-Referenced Scores

The top section of the report presents information about this student's achievement in several different ways. The National Percentile (NP) data and graph indicate how this student performed compared to students of the same grade nationally. The National Percentile range indicates that if this student had taken the test numerous times the scores would have fallen within the range shown. The shaded area on the graph represents the average range of scores, usually defined as the middle 50 percent of students nationally. Scores in the area to the right of the shading are above the average range. Scores in the area to the left of the shading are below the average range.

In Reading, for example, this student achieved a National Percentile rank of 65. This student scored higher than 65 percent of the students nationally. This score is in the average range. This student has a total of five scores in the average range. One score is in the above average range. No scores are in the below average range.

Performance on Objectives

The next section of the report presents performance on the objectives. Each objective is measured by a minimum of 4 items. The Objectives Performance Index (OPI) provides an estimate of the number of items that a student could be expected to answer correctly if there had been 100 items for that objective. The OPI is used to indicate mastery of each objective. An OPI of 75 and above characterizes Mastery. An OPI between 50 and 74 indicates Partial Mastery, and an OPI below 50 indicates Non-Mastery. The two-digit number preceding the objective title identifies the objective, which is fully described in the Teacher's Guide to *TerraNova*. The bands on either side of the diamonds indicate the range within which the student's test scores would fall if the student were tested numerous times.

In Reading, for example, this student could be expected to respond correctly to 91 out of 100 items measuring Basic Understanding. If this student had taken the test numerous times the OPI for this objective would have fallen between 82 and 93.

Teacher Notes

TerraNova

MULTIPLE ASSESSMENTS

Individual Profile Report

MARY BROWN

Grade 7

Purpose

The Observations section of the Individual Profile Report gives teachers and parents information to interpret this report. This page is a narrative description of the data on the other side.

Simulated Data

Birthdate: 09/11/82
Special Codes:
A B C D E F G H I J K L M N O P Q R S T
4 0 2 2 6   1 2 1
Form/Level: A-17

Test Date: 11/01/99   Scoring: PATTERN (IRT)
QM: 08   Norms Date: 1996

Class: PARKER
School: WINFIELD
District: WINFIELD

City/State: WINFIELD, CA

CTB McGraw-Hill

Page 2

Figure 4 (SOURCE: CTB/McGraw-Hill, copyright © 1997. All rights reserved. Reproduced with permission.)

TerraNova

MULTIPLE ASSESSMENTS

Student Performance Level Report

KEN ALLEN

Grade 4

Purpose

This report describes this student's achievement in terms of five performance levels for each content area. The meaning of these levels is described on the back of this page. Performance levels are a new way of describing achievement.

| Simulated Data |

Birthdate: 02/08/86
Special Codes:
A B C D E F G H I J K L M N O P Q R S T
3 5 9 7 3 2   1 1 1
Form/Level: A-14
Test Date: 04/15/97   Scoring: PATTERN (IRT)
QM: 31   Norms Date: 1996

Class: SCHWARZ
School: WINFIELD
District: GREEN VALLEY

City/State: WINFIELD, CA

CTB McGraw-Hill   Page 1

Performance Levels	Reading	Language	Mathematics	Science	Social Studies
5 Advanced					
4 Proficient					
3 Nearing Proficiency	✓	✓			✓
2 Progressing	✓	✓	✓	✓	✓
1 Step 1	✓	✓	✓	✓	✓

Partially Proficient

Observations

Performance level scores provide a measure of what students *can do* in terms of the content and skills assessed by *TerraNova*, and typically found in curricula for Grades 3, 4, and 5. It is desirable to work towards achieving a Level 4 (Proficient) or Level 5 (Advanced) by the end of Grade 5.

The number of check marks indicates the performance level this student reached in each content area. For example, this student reached Level 3 in Reading and Social Studies.

The performance level indicates this student can perform the majority of what is described for that level and even more of what is described for the levels below. The student may also be capable of performing some of the things described in the next higher level, but not enough to have reached that level of performance.

For example, this student can perform the majority of what is described for Level 3 in Reading and even more of what is described for Level 2 and Level 1 in Reading. This student may also be capable of performing some of what is described for Level 4 in Reading.

For each content area look at the skills and knowledge described in the next higher level. These are the competencies this student needs to demonstrate to show academic growth.

CTBID:92123882146001-04-00052-000054
W1 SPLR P1 final:11/09

Figure 5 (SOURCE: CTB/McGraw-Hill, copyright © 1997. All rights reserved. Reproduced with permission.)

Performance Levels (Grades 3, 4, 5)	Reading	Language	Mathematics	Science	Social Studies
5 Advanced	Students use analogies to generalize. They identify a paraphrase of concepts or ideas in texts. They can indicate thought processes that led them to a previous answer. In written responses, they demonstrate understanding of an implied theme, assess intent of passage information, and provide justification as well as support for their answers.	Students understand logical development in paragraph structure. They identify essential information from notes. They recognize the effect of prepositional phrases on subject-verb agreement. They find and correct at least 4 out of 6 errors when editing simple narratives. They correct run-on and incomplete sentences in more complex texts. They can eliminate all errors when editing their own work.	Students locate decimals on a number line; compute with decimals and fractions; read scale drawings; find areas; identify geometric transformations; construct and label bar graphs; find simple probabilities; find averages; use patterns in data to solve problems; use multiple strategies and concepts to solve unfamiliar problems; express mathematical ideas and explain the problem-solving process.	Students understand a broad range of grade level scientific concepts, such as the structure of Earth and instinctive behavior. They know terminology, such as decomposers, fossil fuel, eclipse, and buoyancy. Knowledge of more complex environmental issues includes, for example, the positive consequences of a forest fire. Students can process and interpret more detailed tables and graphs. They can suggest improvements to experimental design, such as running more trials.	Students consistently demonstrate skills such as synthesizing information from two sources (e.g., a document and a map). They show understanding of the democratic process and global environmental issues, and know the location of continents and major countries. They analyze and summarize information from multiple sources in early American history. They thoroughly explain both sides of an issue and give complete and detailed written answers to questions.
4 Proficient	Students interpret figures of speech. They recognize paraphrase of text information and retrieve information to complete forms. In more complex texts, they identify themes, main ideas, or author purpose/point of view. They analyze and apply information in graphic and text form, make reasonable generalizations, and draw conclusions. In written responses, they can identify key elements from text.	Students select the best supporting sentences for a topic sentence. They use compound predicates to combine sentences. They identify simple subjects and predicates, recognize correct usage when confronted with two types of errors, and find and correct at least 3 out of 6 errors when editing simple narratives. They can edit their own work with only minor errors.	Students compare, order, and round whole numbers; know place value to thousands; identify fractions; use computation and estimation strategies; relate multiplication to addition; measure to nearest half-inch and centimeter; measure and find perimeters; estimate measures; find elapsed times; combine and subdivide shapes; identify parallel lines; interpret tables and graphs; solve two-step problems.	Students have a range of specific science knowledge, including details about animal adaptations and classification, states of matter, and the geology of Earth. They recognize scientific words such as habitat, gravity, and mass. They understand the usefulness of computers. They understand reasons for conserving natural resources. Understanding of experimentation includes analyzing purpose, interpreting data, and selecting tools to gather data.	Students demonstrate skills such as making inferences, using historical documents and analyzing maps to determine the economic strengths of a region. They understand the function of currency in various cultures and supply and demand. They summarize information from multiple sources, recognize relationships, determine relevance of information, and show global awareness. They propose solutions to real-world problems and support ideas with appropriate details.
3 Nearing Proficiency	Students use context clues and structural analysis to determine word meaning. They recognize homonyms and antonyms in grade-level text. They identify important details, sequence, cause and effect, and lessons embedded in the text. They interpret characters' feelings and apply information to new situations. In written responses, they can express an opinion and support it.	Students identify irrelevant sentences in paragraphs and select the best place to insert new information. They recognize faulty sentence construction. They combine simple sentences with conjunctions and use simple subordination of phrases/clauses. They recognize correct conventions for dates, closings, and place names in informal correspondence.	Students identify even and odd numbers; subtract whole numbers with regrouping; multiply and divide by one-digit numbers; identify simple fractions; measure with ruler to nearest inch; tell time to nearest fifteen minutes; recognize and classify common shapes; recognize symmetry; subdivide shapes; complete bar graphs; extend numerical and geometric patterns; apply simple logical reasoning.	Students are familiar with the life cycles of plants and animals. They can identify an example of a cold-blooded animal. They infer what once existed from fossil evidence. They recognize the term habitat. They understand the water cycle. They know science and society issues such as recycling and sources of pollution. They can sequence technological advances. They extrapolate data, devise a simple classification scheme, and determine the purpose of a simple experiment.	Students demonstrate skills in organizing information. They use time lines, product and global maps, and cardinal directions. They understand simple cause and effect relationships and historical documents. They sequence events, associate natural resources. They compare life in different times and understand some economic concepts related to products, jobs, and the environment. They give some detail in written responses.
2 Progressing	Students identify synonyms for grade-level words, and use context clues to define common words. They make simple inferences and predictions based on text. They identify characters' feelings. They can transfer information from text to graphic form, or from graphic form to text. In written responses, they can provide limited support for their answers.	Students identify the use of correct verb tenses and supply verbs to complete sentences. They complete paragraphs by selecting an appropriate topic sentence. They select correct adjective forms.	Students know ordinal numbers; solve coin combination problems; count by tens; add whole numbers with regrouping; have basic estimation skills; understand addition property of zero; write and identify number sentences describing simple situations; read calendars; identify appropriate measurement tools; recognize congruent figures; use simple coordinate grids; read common tables and graphs.	Students recognize that plants decompose and become part of soil. They can classify a plant as a vegetable. They recognize that camouflage relates to survival. They recognize terms such as hibernate. They have an understanding of human impact on the environment and are familiar with causes of pollution. They find the correct bar graph to represent given data and transfer data appropriate for middle elementary grades to a bar graph.	Students demonstrate simple information-processing skills such as using basic maps and keys. They recognize simple geographical terms, types of jobs, modes of transportation, and natural resources. They connect a human need with an appropriate community service. They identify some early famous presidents and know the capital of the United States. Their written answers are partially complete.
1 Step 1	Students select pictured representations of ideas and identify stated details contained in simple texts. In written responses, they can select and transfer information from charts.	Students supply subjects to complete sentences. They identify the correct use of pronouns. They edit for the correct use of end marks and initial capital letters, and identify the correct convention for greetings in letters.	Students read and recognize numbers to 1000; identify real-world use of numbers; add and subtract two-digit numbers without regrouping; identify addition situations; recognize and complete simple geometric and numerical patterns.	Students recognize basic adaptations for living in the water, identify an animal that is hatched from an egg, and associate an organism with its correct environment. They identify an object as metal. They have some understanding of conditions on the moon. They supply one way a computer can be useful. They associate an instrument like a telescope with a field of study.	Students are developing fundamental social studies skills such as locating and classifying basic information. They locate information in pictures and read and complete simple bar graphs related to social studies concepts and contexts. They can connect some city buildings with their functions and recognize certain historical objects.

Partially Proficient

W1 SPLR P2:11/02

IMPORTANT: Each performance level, depicted on the other side, indicates the student can perform the majority of what is described for that level and even more of what is described for the levels below. The student may also be capable of performing some of the things described in the next higher level, but not enough to have reached that level.

Figure 6 (SOURCE: CTB/McGraw-Hill, copyright © 1997. All rights reserved. Reproduced with permission.)

confidence interval. In these reports, we usually report either a 90 percent or 95 percent confidence interval. Interpret a confidence interval this way: Suppose we report a 90 percent confidence interval of 25 to 37. This means we estimate that, if the child took the test multiple times, we would expect that child's score to be in the 25 to 37 range 90 percent of the time.

Now look under the section titled Norm-Referenced Scores on the first page of the Individual Profile Report (Figure 3). The farthest column on the right provides the NP Range, which is the National Percentile scores represented by the score bands in the chart.

Next notice the column labeled Grade Equivalent. Theoretically, grade level equivalents equate a student's score in a skill area with the average grade placement of children who made the same score. Many psychologists and test developers would prefer that we stopped reporting grade equivalents, because they can be grossly misleading. For example, the average reading grade level of high school seniors as reported by one of the more popular tests is the eighth grade level. Does that mean that the nation's high school seniors cannot read? No. The way the test publisher calculated grade equivalents was to determine the average test scores for students in grades 4 to 6 and then simply extend the resulting prediction formula to grades 7 to 12. The result is that parents of average high school seniors who take the test in question would mistakenly believe that their seniors are reading four grade levels behind! Stick to the percentile in interpreting your child's scores.

Now look at the columns labeled Scale Score and National Stanine. These are two of a group of scores we also call *standard scores.* In reports for other tests, you may see other standard scores reported, such as Normal Curve Equivalents (NCEs), Z-Scores, and T-Scores. The IQ that we report on intelligence tests, for example, is a standard score. Standard scores are simply a way of expressing a student's scores in terms of the statistical properties of the scores from the norm group against which we are comparing the child. Although most psychologists prefer to speak in terms of standard scores among themselves, parents are advised to stick to percentiles in interpreting your child's performance.

Now look at the section of the report labeled Performance on Objectives. In this section, the test publisher reports how your child did on the various skills that make up each skills area. Note that the scores on each objective are expressed as a percentile band, and you are again told whether your child's score constitutes mastery, non-mastery, or partial mastery. Note that these scores are made up of tallies of sometimes small numbers of test items taken from sections such as Reading or Math. Because they are calculated from a much smaller number of scores than the main scales are (for example, Sentence Comprehension is made up of fewer items than overall Reading), their scores are less reliable than those of the main scales.

Now look at the second page of the Individual Profile Report (Figure 4). Here the test publisher provides a narrative summary of how the child did on the test. These summaries are computer-generated according to rules provided by the publisher. Note that the results descriptions are more general than those on the previous three report pages. But they allow the teacher to form a general picture of which students are performing at what general skill levels.

Finally, your child's guidance counselor may receive a summary report such as the TerraNova Student Performance Level Report. (See Figures 5 and 6.) In this report, the publisher explains to school personnel what skills the test assessed and generally how proficiently the child tested under each skill.

Which States Require Which Tests

Tables 1 through 3 summarize standardized testing practices in the 50 states and the District of Columbia. This information is constantly changing; the information presented here was accurate as of the date of printing of this book. Many states have changed their testing practices in response to revised accountability legislation, while others have changed the tests they use.

Table 1   State Web Sites: Education and Testing

STATE	GENERAL WEB SITE	STATE TESTING WEB SITE
Alabama	http://www.alsde.edu/	http://www.fairtest.org/states/al.htm
Alaska	www.educ.state.ak.us/	http://www.educ.state.ak.us/
Arizona	http://www.ade.state.az.us/	http://www.ade.state.az.us/standards/
Arkansas	http://arkedu.k12.ar.us/	http://www.fairtest.org/states/ar.htm
California	http://goldmine.cde.ca.gov/	http://star.cde.ca.gov/
Colorado	http://www.cde.state.co.us/index_home.htm	http://www.cde.state.co.us/index_assess.htm
Connecticut	http://www.state.ct.us/sde/	http://www.state.ct.us/sde/cmt/index.htm
Delaware	http://www.doe.state.de.us/	http://www.doe.state.de.us/aab/index.htm
District of Columbia	http://www.k12.dc.us/dcps/home.html	http://www.k12.dc.us/dcps/data/data_frame2.html
Florida	http://www.firn.edu/doe/	http://www.firn.edu/doe/sas/sasshome.htm
Georgia	http://www.doe.k12.ga.us/	http://www.doe.k12.ga.us/sla/ret/recotest.html
Hawaii	http://kalama.doe.hawaii.edu/upena/	http://www.fairtest.org/states/hi.htm
Idaho	http://www.sde.state.id.us/Dept/	http://www.sde.state.id.us/instruct/ schoolaccount/statetesting.htm
Illinois	http://www.isbe.state.il.us/	http://www.isbe.state.il.us/isat/
Indiana	http://doe.state.in.us/	http://doe.state.in.us/assessment/welcome.html
Iowa	http://www.state.ia.us/educate/index.html	(Tests Chosen Locally)
Kansas	http://www.ksbe.state.ks.us/	http://www.ksbe.state.ks.us/assessment/
Kentucky	htp://www.kde.state.ky.us/	http://www.kde.state.ky.us/oaa/
Louisiana	http://www.doe.state.la.us/DOE/asps/home.asp	http://www.doe.state.la.us/DOE/asps/home.asp? I=HISTAKES
Maine	http://janus.state.me.us/education/homepage.htm	http://janus.state.me.us/education/mea/ meacompass.htm
Maryland	http://www.msde.state.md.us/	http://msp.msde.state.md.us/
Massachusetts	http://www.doe.mass.edu/	http://www.doe.mass.edu/mcas/
Michigan	http://www.mde.state.mi.us/	http://www.MeritAward.state.mi.us/merit/meap/ index.htm

STATE	GENERAL WEB SITE	STATE TESTING WEB SITE
Minnesota	http://www.educ.state.mn.us/	http://fairtest.org/states/mn.htm
Mississippi	http://mdek12.state.ms.us/	http://fairtest.org/states/ms.htm
Missouri	http://services.dese.state.mo.us/	http://fairtest.org/states/mo.htm
Montana	http://www.metnet.state.mt.us/	http://fairtest.org/states/mt.htm
Nebraska	http://www.nde.state.ne.us/	http://www.edneb.org/IPS/AppAccrd/ ApprAccrd.html
Nevada	http://www.nde.state.nv.us/	http://www.nsn.k12.nv.us/nvdoe/reports/ TerraNova.doc
New Hampshire	http://www.state.nh.us/doe/	http://www.state.nh.us/doe/Assessment/ assessme(NHEIAP).htm
New Jersey	http://www.state.nj.us/education/	http://www.state.nj.us/njded/stass/index.html
New Mexico	http://sde.state.nm.us/	http://sde.state.nm.us/press/august30a.html
New York	http://www.nysed.gov/	http://www.emsc.nysed.gov/ciai/assess.html
North Carolina	http://www.dpi.state.nc.us/	http://www.dpi.state.nc.us/accountability/ reporting/index.html
North Dakota	http://www.dpi.state.nd.us/dpi/index.htm	http://www.dpi.state.nd.us/dpi/reports/ assess/assess.htm
Ohio	http://www.ode.state.oh.us/	http://www.ode.state.oh.us/ca/
Oklahoma	http://sde.state.ok.us/	http://sde.state.ok.us/acrob/testpack.pdf
Oregon	http://www.ode.state.or.us//	http://www.ode.state.or.us//asmt/index.htm
Pennsylvania	http://www.pde.psu.edu/	http://www.fairtest.org/states/pa.htm
Rhode Island	http://www.ridoe.net/	http://www.ridoe.net/standards/default.htm
South Carolina	http://www.state.sc.us/sde/	http://www.state.sc.us/sde/reports/terranov.htm
South Dakota	http://www.state.sd.us/state/executive/deca/	http://www.state.sd.us/state/executive/deca/TA/ McRelReport/McRelReports.htm
Tennessee	http://www.state.tn.us/education/	http://www.state.tn.us/education/tsintro.htm
Texas	http://www.tea.state.tx.us/	http://www.tea.state.tx.us/student.assessment/
Utah	http://www.usoe.k12.ut.us/	http://www.usoe.k12.ut.us/eval/usoeeval.htm
Vermont	http://www.state.vt.us/educ/	http://www.fairtest.org/states/vt.htm

STATE	GENERAL WEB SITE	STATE TESTING WEB SITE
Virginia	http://www.pen.k12.va.us/Anthology/VDOE/	http://www.pen.k12.va.us/VDOE/Assessment/home.shtml
Washington	http://www.k12.wa.us/	http://www.k12.wa.us/assessment/
West Virginia	http://wvde.state.wv.us/	http://wvde.state.wv.us/
Wisconsin	http://www.dpi.state.wi.us/	http://www.dpi.state.wi.us/dpi/dltcl/eis/achfacts.html
Wyoming	http://www.k12.wy.us/wdehome.html	http://www.asme.com/wycas/index.htm

Table 2 Norm-Referenced and Criterion-Referenced Tests Administered by State

STATE	NORM-REFERENCED TEST	CRITERION-REFERENCED TEST	EXIT EXAM
Alabama	Stanford Achievement Test		Alabama High School Graduation Exam
Alaska	California Achievement Test	Alaska Benchmark Examinations	
Arizona	Stanford Achievement Test	Arizona's Instrument to Measure Standards (AIMS)	
Arkansas	Stanford Achievement Test		
California	Stanford Achievement Test	Standardized Testing and Reporting Supplement	High School Exit Exam (HSEE)
Colorado	None	Colorado Student Assessment Program	
Connecticut		Connecticut Mastery Test	
Delaware	Stanford Achievement Test	Delaware Student Testing Program	
District of Columbia	Stanford Achievement Test		
Florida	(Locally Selected)	Florida Comprehensive Assessment Test (FCAT)	High School Competency Test (HSCT)
Georgia	Stanford Achievement Test	Georgia Kindergarten Assessment Program—Revised and Criterion-Referenced Competency Tests (CRCT)	Georgia High School Graduation Tests
Hawaii	Stanford Achievement Test	Credit by Examination	Hawaii State Test of Essential Competencies
Idaho	Iowa Tests of Basic Skills/ Tests of Achievement and Proficiency	Direct Writing/Mathematics Assessment, Idaho Reading Indicator	
Illinois		Illinois Standards Achievement Tests	Prairie State Achievement Examination
Indiana		Indiana Statewide Testing for Educational Progress	
Iowa	(None)		
Kansas		(State-Developed Tests)	
Kentucky	Comprehensive Test of Basic Skills	Kentucky Core Content Tests	
Louisiana	Iowa Tests of Basic Skills	Louisiana Educational Assessment Program	Graduate Exit Exam
Maine		Maine Educational Assessment	High School Assessment Test
Maryland		Maryland School Performance Assessment Program, Maryland Functional Testing Program	

STATE	NORM-REFERENCED TEST	CRITERION-REFERENCED TEST	EXIT EXAM
Massachusetts		Massachusetts Comprehensive Assessment System	
Michigan		Michigan Educational Assessment Program	High School Test
Minnesota		Basic Standards Test	Profile of Learning
Mississippi	Comprehensive Test of Basic Skills	Subject Area Testing Program	Functional Literacy Examination
Missouri		Missouri Mastery and Achievement Test	
Montana	Iowa Tests of Basic Skills		
Nebraska			
Nevada	TerraNova		Nevada High School Proficiency Examination
New Hampshire		NH Educational Improvement and Assessment Program	
New Jersey		Elementary School Proficiency Test/Early Warning Test	High School Proficiency Test
New Mexico	TerraNova		New Mexico High School Competency Exam
New York		Pupil Evaluation Program/ Preliminary Competency Tests	Regents Competency Tests
North Carolina	Iowa Tests of Basic Skills	NC End of Grade Test	
North Dakota	TerraNova	ND Reading, Writing, Speaking, Listening, Math Test	
Ohio		Ohio Proficiency Tests	Ohio Proficiency Tests
Oklahoma	Iowa Tests of Basic Skills	Oklahoma Criterion-Referenced Tests	
Oregon		Oregon Statewide Assessment	
Pennsylvania		Pennsylvania System of School Assessment	
Rhode Island	Metropolitan Achievement Test	New Standards English Language Arts Reference Exam, New Standards Mathematics Reference Exam, Rhode Island Writing Assessment, and Rhode Island Health Education Assessment	
South Carolina	TerraNova	Palmetto Achievement Challenge Tests	High School Exit Exam
South Dakota	Stanford Achievement Test		
Tennessee	Tennessee Comprehensive Assessment Program	Tennessee Comprehensive Assessment Program	

STATE	NORM-REFERENCED TEST	CRITERION-REFERENCED TEST	EXIT EXAM
Texas		Texas Assessment of Academic Skills, End-of-Course Examinations	Texas Assessment of Academic Skills
Utah	Stanford Achievement Test	Core Curriculum Testing	
Vermont		New Standards Reference Exams	
Virginia	Stanford Achievement Test	Virginia Standards of Learning	Virginia Standards of Learning
Washington	Iowa Tests of Basic Skills	Washington Assessment of Student Learning	Washington Assessment of Student Learning
West Virginia	Stanford Achievement Test		
Wisconsin	TerraNova	Wisconsin Knowledge and Concepts Examinations	
Wyoming	TerraNova	Wyoming Comprehensive Assessment System	Wyoming Comprehensive Assessment System

Table 3   Standardized Test Schedules by State

STATE	KG	1	2	3	4	5	6	7	8	9	10	11	12	COMMENT
Alabama				X	X	X	X	X	X	X	X	X	X	
Alaska				X	X		X		X			X		
Arizona			X	X	X	X	X	X	X	X	X	X	X	
Arkansas					X	X		X	X		X	X	X	
California			X	X	X	X	X	X	X	X	X	X		
Colorado				X	X	X		X	X					
Connecticut					X		X		X					
Delaware				X	X	X			X		X	X		
District of Columbia		X	X	X	X	X	X	X	X	X	X	X		
Florida				X	X	X			X		X			There is no state-mandated norm-referenced testing. However, the state collects information furnished by local districts that elect to perform norm-referenced testing. The FCAT is administered to Grades 4, 8, and 10 to assess reading and Grades 5, 8, and 10 to assess math.
Georgia	X			X	X	X	X		X			X		
Hawaii				X			X		X		X			The Credit by Examination is voluntary and is given in Grade 8 in Algebra and Foreign Languages.
Idaho				X	X	X	X	X	X	X	X	X		
Illinois				X	X	X		X	X		X	X		Exit Exam failure will not disqualify students from graduation if all other requirements are met.
Indiana				X			X		X		X			
Iowa		*	*	*	*	*	*	*	*	*	*	*	*	*Iowa does not currently have a statewide testing program. Locally chosen assessments are administered to grades determined locally.
Kansas				X	X	X		X	X		X	X		

STATE	KG	1	2	3	4	5	6	7	8	9	10	11	12	COMMENT
Kentucky					X	X	X	X	X	X	X	X	X	
Louisiana				X	X	X	X	X	X	X	X	X	X	
Maine					X				X			X		
Maryland				X		X			X	X	X	X	X	
Massachusetts				X	X	X		X	X	X	X			
Michigan					X	X		X	X					
Minnesota				X		X			X	X	X	X	X	
Mississippi				X	X	X	X	X	X					Mississippi officials would not return phone calls or emails regarding this information.
Missouri			X	X	X	X	X	X	X	X	X			
Montana					X				X			X		The State Board of Education has decided to use a single norm-referenced test statewide beginning 2000–2001 school year.
Nebraska		**	**	**	**	**	**	**	**	**	**	**	**	**Decisions regarding testing are left to the individual school districts.
Nevada					X				X					Districts choose whether and how to test with norm-referenced tests.
New Hampshire				X			X				X			
New Jersey				X	X			X	X	X	X	X		
New Mexico					X		X		X					
New York				X	X	X	X	X	X	X			X	Assessment program is going through major revisions.
North Carolina	X			X	X	X	X		X	X			X	NRT Testing selects samples of students, not all.
North Dakota					X		X		X		X			
Ohio					X		X			X			X	
Oklahoma				X		X		X	X			X		
Oregon				X		X			X		X			

STATE	KG	1	2	3	4	5	6	7	8	9	10	11	12	COMMENT
Pennsylvania						X	X		X	X		X		
Rhode Island				X	X	X		X	X	X	X	X		
South Carolina				X	X	X	X	X	X	X	X	***	***	***Students who fail the High School Exit Exam have opportunities to take the exam again in grades 11 and 12.
South Dakota			X		X	X			X	X		X		
Tennessee			X	X	X	X	X	X	X					
Texas				X	X	X	X	X	X		X	X	X	
Utah		X	X	X	X	X	X	X	X	X	X	X	X	
Vermont					X	X	X		X	X	X	X		Rated by the Centers for Fair and Open Testing as a nearly model system for assessment.
Virginia				X	X	X	X		X	X		X		
Washington					X			X			X			
West Virginia				X	X	X	X	X	X	X	X	X		
Wisconsin					X				X		X			
Wyoming					X				X			X		

Testing Accommodations

The more testing procedures vary from one classroom or school to the next, the less we can compare the scores from one group to another. Consider a test in which the publisher recommends that three sections of the test be given in one 45-minute session per day on three consecutive days. School A follows those directions. To save time, School B gives all three sections of the test in one session lasting slightly more than two hours. We can't say that both schools followed the same testing procedures. Remember that the test publishers provide testing procedures so schools can administer the tests in as close a manner as possible to the way the tests were administered to the groups used to obtain test norms. When we compare students' scores to norms, we want to compare apples to apples, not apples to oranges.

Most schools justifiably resist making any changes in testing procedures. Informally, a teacher can make minor changes that don't alter the testing procedures, such as separating two students who talk with each other instead of paying attention to the test; letting Lisa, who is getting over an ear infection, sit closer to the front so she can hear better; or moving Jeffrey away from the window to prevent his looking out the window and daydreaming.

There are two groups of students who require more formal testing accommodations. One group of students is identified as having a disability under Section 504 of the Rehabilitation Act of 1973 (Public Law 93-112). These students face some challenge but, with reasonable and appropriate accommodation, can take advantage of the same educational opportunities as other students. That is, they have a condition that requires some accommodation for them.

Just as schools must remove physical barriers to accommodate students with disabilities, they must make appropriate accommodations to remove other types of barriers to students' access to education. Marie is profoundly deaf, even with strong hearing aids. She does well in school with the aid of an interpreter, who signs her teacher's instructions to her and tells her teacher what Marie says in reply. An appropriate accommodation for Marie would be to provide the interpreter to sign test instructions to her, or to allow her to watch a videotape with an interpreter signing test instructions. Such a reasonable accommodation would not deviate from standard testing procedures and, in fact, would ensure that Marie received the same instructions as the other students.

If your child is considered disabled and has what is generally called a Section 504 Plan or individual accommodation plan (IAP), then the appropriate way to ask for testing accommodations is to ask for them in a meeting to discuss school accommodations under the plan. If your child is not already covered by such a plan, he or she won't qualify for one merely because you request testing accommodations.

The other group of students who may receive formal testing accommodations are those identified as handicapped under the Individuals with Disabilities Education Act (IDEA)—students with mental retardation, learning disabilities, serious emotional disturbance, orthopedic handicap, hearing or visual problems, and other handicaps defined in the law. These students have been identified under procedures governed by federal and sometimes state law, and their education is governed by a document called the Individualized Educational Program (IEP). Unless you are under a court order specifically revoking your educational rights on behalf of your child, you are a full member of the IEP team even if you and your child's other parent are divorced and the other parent has custody. Until recently, IEP teams actually had the prerogative to exclude certain handicapped students from taking standardized group testing altogether. However, today states make it more difficult to exclude students from testing.

If your child is classified as handicapped and has an IEP, the appropriate place to ask for testing accommodations is in an IEP team meeting. In fact, federal regulations require IEP teams to address testing accommodations. You have the right to call a meeting at any time. In that meeting, you will have the opportunity to present your case for the accommodations you believe are necessary. Be prepared for the other team members to resist making extreme accommodations unless you can present a very strong case. If your child is identified as handicapped and you believe that he or she should be provided special testing accommodations, contact the person at your child's school who is responsible for convening IEP meetings and request a meeting to discuss testing accommodations.

Problems arise when a request is made for accommodations that cause major departures from standard testing procedures. For example, Lynn has an identified learning disability in mathematics calculation and attends resource classes for math. Her disability is so severe that her IEP calls for her to use a calculator when performing all math problems. She fully understands math concepts, but she simply can't perform the calculations without the aid of a calculator. Now it's time for Lynn to take the school-based standardized tests, and she asks to use a calculator. In this case, since her IEP already requires her to be provided with a calculator when performing math calculations, she may be allowed a calculator during school standardized tests. However, because using a calculator constitutes a major violation of standard testing procedures, her score on all sections in which she is allowed to use a calculator will be recorded as a failure, and her results in some states will be removed from among those of other students in her school in calculating school results.

How do we determine whether a student is allowed formal accommodations in standardized school testing and what these accommodations may be? First, if your child is not already identified as either handicapped or disabled, having the child classified in either group solely to receive testing accommodations will be considered a violation of the laws governing both classifications. Second, even if your child is already classified in either group, your state's department of public instruction will provide strict guidelines for the testing accommodations schools may make. Third, even if your child is classified in either group and you are proposing testing accommodations allowed under state testing guidelines, any accommodations must still be both *reasonable* and *appropriate*. To be reasonable and appropriate, testing accommodations must relate to your child's disability and must be similar to those already in place in his or her daily educational program. If your child is always tested individually in a separate room for all tests in all subjects, then a similar practice in taking school-based standardized tests may be appropriate. But if your child has a learning disability only in mathematics calculation, requesting that all test questions be read to him or her is inappropriate because that accommodation does not relate to his identified handicap.

Glossary

Accountability The idea that a school district is held responsible for the achievement of its students. The term may also be applied to holding students responsible for a certain level of achievement in order to be promoted or to graduate.

Achievement test An assessment that measures current knowledge in one or more of the areas taught in most schools, such as reading, math, and language arts.

Aptitude test An assessment designed to predict a student's potential for learning knowledge or skills.

Content validity The extent to which a test represents the content it is designed to cover.

Criterion-referenced test A test that rates how thoroughly a student has mastered a specific skill or area of knowledge. Typically, a criterion-referenced test is subjective, and relies on someone to observe and rate student work; it doesn't allow for easy comparisons of achievement among students. Performance assessments are criterion-referenced tests. The opposite of a criterion-referenced test is a norm-referenced test.

Frequency distribution A tabulation of individual scores (or groups of scores) that shows the number of persons who obtained each score.

Generalizability The idea that the score on a test reflects what a child knows about a subject, or how well he performs the skills the test is supposed to be assessing. Generalizability requires that enough test items are administered to truly assess a student's achievement.

Grade equivalent A score on a scale developed to indicate the school grade (usually measured in months of a year) that corresponds to an average chronological age, mental age, test score, or other characteristic. A grade equivalent of 6.4 is interpreted as a score that is average for a group in the fourth month of Grade 6.

High-stakes assessment A type of standardized test that has major consequences for a student or school (such as whether a child graduates from high school or gets admitted to college).

Mean Average score of a group of scores.

Median The middle score in a set of scores ranked from smallest to largest.

National percentile Percentile score derived from the performance of a group of individuals across the nation.

Normative sample A comparison group consisting of individuals who have taken a test under standard conditions.

Norm-referenced test A standardized test that can compare scores of students in one school with a reference group (usually other students in the same grade and age, called the "norm group"). Norm-referenced tests compare the achievement of one student or the students of a school, school district, or state with the norm score.

Norms A summary of the performance of a group of individuals on which a test was standardized.

Percentile An incorrect form of the word *centile,* which is the percent of a group of scores that falls below a given score. Although the correct term is *centile,* much of the testing literature has adopted the term *percentile.*

Performance standards A level of performance on a test set by education experts.

Quartiles Points that divide the frequency distribution of scores into equal fourths.

Regression to the mean The tendency of scores in a group of scores to vary in the direction of the mean. For example: If a child has an abnormally low score on a test, she is likely to make a higher score (that is, one closer to the mean) the next time she takes the test.

Reliability The consistency with which a test measures some trait or characteristic. A measure can be reliable without being valid, but it can't be valid without being reliable.

Standard deviation A statistical measure used to describe the extent to which scores vary in a group of scores. Approximately 68 percent of scores in a group are expected to be in a range from one standard deviation below the mean to one standard deviation above the mean.

Standardized test A test that contains well-defined questions of proven validity and that produces reliable scores. Such tests are commonly paper-and-pencil exams containing multiple-choice items, true or false questions, matching exercises, or short fill-in-the-blanks items. These tests may also include performance assessment items (such as a writing sample), but assessment items cannot be completed quickly or scored reliably.

Test anxiety Anxiety that occurs in test-taking situations. Test anxiety can seriously impair individuals' ability to obtain accurate scores on a test.

Validity The extent to which a test measures the trait or characteristic it is designed to measure. Also see *reliability.*

Answer Keys for Practice Skills

Chapter 2: Vocabulary

1. C
2. C
3. D
4. C
5. C
6. B
7. D
8. A
9. D
10. B
11. A

Chapter 3: Word Meanings in Context

1. A
2. D
3. B
4. C
5. B
6. A
7. B
8. C
9. D
10. A
11. C
12. B
13. D
14. B
15. C
16. C

17. B
18. A
19. D
20. C
21. C

Chapter 4: Synonyms, Antonyms, and Homonyms

1. B
2. C
3. C
4. A
5. C
6. D
7. A
8. D
9. B
10. C
11. A
12. C
13. C
14. A
15. C
16. D
17. B

Chapter 5: Word Sounds

1. C
2. A
3. C

4. B
5. A
6. C
7. A
8. D
9. A
10. A
11. D
12. D
13. A
14. D
15. C
16. A
17. D
18. D
19. A
20. D
21. C
22. D
23. A
24. B
25. B
26. C
27. D

Chapter 6: Word Recognition

1. B
2. B
3. C
4. C
5. D
6. D

7. C
8. B
9. A
10. C
11. D
12. C
13. B
14. B
15. C
16. B
17. D
18. D
19. A

Chapter 7: Spelling

1. C
2. D
3. B
4. C
5. C
6. B
7. A
8. C
9. C
10. A
11. D
12. C
13. C
14. A
15. C
16. A
17. D

18	B
19	D
20	D
21	B

**Chapter 8:
Capitalization and
Punctuation**

1	A
2	D
3	D
4	A
5	B
6	A
7	D
8	A
9	C
10	B
11	D
12	B
13	D
14	A
15	A
16	C
17	D
18	B
19	B
20	B
21	D
22	A
23	C

**Chapter 9:
Grammar Skills**

1	D
2	B
3	A
4	B
5	C
6	C
7	D
8	A
9	B
10	D
11	D
12	D
13	C
14	D
15	B
16	A

**Chapter 10:
Breaking It Down**

1	C
2	B
3	C
4	B
5	D
6	B
7	A
8	B
9	B
10	A

11	D
12	D
13	D
14	C
15	B
16	B

**Chapter 11:
Reading
Comprehension**

1	B
2	C
3	A
4	D
5	A
6	B
7	D
8	D
9	D
10	C
11	A
12	B
13	D
14	A

**Chapter 12:
Literary Genres**

1	C
2	D
3	C
4	B

5	A
6	C
7	A
8	D
9	B
10	C
11	A
12	C
13	B
14	C
15	D

**Chapter 13:
Study Skills**

1	B
2	B
3	A
4	A
5	A
6	D
7	A
8	C
9	D
10	C
11	A
12	B
13	A
14	D
15	B
16	A

Sample Practice Test

You may be riding a roller coaster of feelings and opinions at this point. If your child has gone through the preceding chapters easily, then you're both probably excited to move on, to jump in with both feet, take the test, and that will be that. On the other hand, your child may have struggled a bit with some of the chapters. Some of the concepts may be difficult for him and will require a little more practice. Never fear!

All children acquire skills in all areas of learning when they are developmentally ready. We can't push them, but we can reinforce the skills they already know. In addition, we can play games and do activities to pave the way for their understanding of the skills that they will need to master later. With luck, that's what you've done with the preceding chapters.

The test that follows is designed to incorporate components of several different kinds of standardized tests. The test that your child takes in school probably won't look just like this one, but it should be sufficiently similar that he should be pretty comfortable with the format. The administration of tests varies as well. It is important that your child hear the rhythm and language used in standardized tests. If you wish, you may have your child read the directions that precede each test section to you first and explain what the item is asking him to do. Your child may try it on his own if you feel he understands it, or you may want to clarify the instructions.

Test Administration

If you like, you may complete the entire test in one day, but it is not recommended that your child attempt to finish it in one sitting. As test administrator, you'll find that you'll need to stretch, have a snack, or use the bathroom too! If you plan to do the test in one day, leave at least 15 minutes between sessions.

Before you start, prepare a quiet place, free of distractions. Have two or three sharpened pencils with erasers that don't smudge and a flat, clear work space. As your child proceeds from item to item, encourage him to ask if he doesn't understand something. In a real testing situation, questions are accepted, but the extent to which items can be explained is limited. Don't go overboard in making sure your child understands what to do. Your child will have to learn to trust his instincts somewhat.

The test shouldn't take all day. If your youngster seems to be dawdling along, enforce time limits and help him to understand that the real test will have time limits as well. Relax, and try to have fun!

To the Student:

These tests will give you a chance to put the tips you have learned to work. A few last reminders . . .

- Be sure you understand all the directions before you begin each test. You may ask the teacher questions about the directions if you do not understand them.

- Work as quickly as you can during each test.

- When you change an answer, be sure to erase your first mark completely.

- You can guess at an answer or skip difficult items and go back to them later.

- Use the tips you have learned whenever you can.

- It is OK to be a little nervous. You may even do better.

Now that you have completed the lessons in this book, you are on your way to scoring high!

STUDENT'S NAME

LAST | FIRST | MI

SCHOOL

TEACHER

FEMALE ○   MALE ○

BIRTHDATE

MONTH	DAY	YEAR

JAN, FEB, MAR, APR, MAY, JUN, JUL, AUG, SEP, OCT, NOV, DEC

GRADE
① ② ③ ④ ⑤ ⑥

Vocabulary

1 Ⓐ Ⓑ Ⓒ Ⓓ 2 Ⓐ Ⓑ Ⓒ Ⓓ 3 Ⓐ Ⓑ Ⓒ Ⓓ 4 Ⓐ Ⓑ Ⓒ Ⓓ

Picture Vocabulary

5 Ⓐ Ⓑ Ⓒ Ⓓ 6 Ⓐ Ⓑ Ⓒ Ⓓ 7 Ⓐ Ⓑ Ⓒ Ⓓ 8 Ⓐ Ⓑ Ⓒ Ⓓ 9 Ⓐ Ⓑ Ⓒ Ⓓ

Words in Context

10 Ⓐ Ⓑ Ⓒ Ⓓ 14 Ⓐ Ⓑ Ⓒ Ⓓ 17 Ⓐ Ⓑ Ⓒ Ⓓ 20 Ⓐ Ⓑ Ⓒ Ⓓ 23 Ⓐ Ⓑ Ⓒ Ⓓ 26 Ⓐ Ⓑ Ⓒ Ⓓ
11 Ⓐ Ⓑ Ⓒ Ⓓ 15 Ⓐ Ⓑ Ⓒ Ⓓ 18 Ⓐ Ⓑ Ⓒ Ⓓ 21 Ⓐ Ⓑ Ⓒ Ⓓ 24 Ⓐ Ⓑ Ⓒ Ⓓ 27 Ⓐ Ⓑ Ⓒ Ⓓ
12 Ⓐ Ⓑ Ⓒ Ⓓ 16 Ⓐ Ⓑ Ⓒ Ⓓ 19 Ⓐ Ⓑ Ⓒ Ⓓ 22 Ⓐ Ⓑ Ⓒ Ⓓ 25 Ⓐ Ⓑ Ⓒ Ⓓ 28 Ⓐ Ⓑ Ⓒ Ⓓ
13 Ⓐ Ⓑ Ⓒ Ⓓ

Synonyms, Antonyms, and Homonyms

29 Ⓐ Ⓑ Ⓒ Ⓓ 32 Ⓐ Ⓑ Ⓒ Ⓓ 35 Ⓐ Ⓑ Ⓒ Ⓓ 38 Ⓐ Ⓑ Ⓒ Ⓓ 40 Ⓐ Ⓑ Ⓒ Ⓓ 42 Ⓐ Ⓑ Ⓒ Ⓓ
30 Ⓐ Ⓑ Ⓒ Ⓓ 33 Ⓐ Ⓑ Ⓒ Ⓓ 36 Ⓐ Ⓑ Ⓒ Ⓓ 39 Ⓐ Ⓑ Ⓒ Ⓓ 41 Ⓐ Ⓑ Ⓒ Ⓓ 43 Ⓐ Ⓑ Ⓒ Ⓓ
31 Ⓐ Ⓑ Ⓒ Ⓓ 34 Ⓐ Ⓑ Ⓒ Ⓓ 37 Ⓐ Ⓑ Ⓒ Ⓓ

Word Sounds

44 Ⓐ Ⓑ Ⓒ Ⓓ 49 Ⓐ Ⓑ Ⓒ Ⓓ 54 Ⓐ Ⓑ Ⓒ Ⓓ 59 Ⓐ Ⓑ Ⓒ Ⓓ 63 Ⓐ Ⓑ Ⓒ Ⓓ 67 Ⓐ Ⓑ Ⓒ Ⓓ
45 Ⓐ Ⓑ Ⓒ Ⓓ 50 Ⓐ Ⓑ Ⓒ Ⓓ 55 Ⓐ Ⓑ Ⓒ Ⓓ 60 Ⓐ Ⓑ Ⓒ Ⓓ 64 Ⓐ Ⓑ Ⓒ Ⓓ 68 Ⓐ Ⓑ Ⓒ Ⓓ
46 Ⓐ Ⓑ Ⓒ Ⓓ 51 Ⓐ Ⓑ Ⓒ Ⓓ 56 Ⓐ Ⓑ Ⓒ Ⓓ 61 Ⓐ Ⓑ Ⓒ Ⓓ 65 Ⓐ Ⓑ Ⓒ Ⓓ 69 Ⓐ Ⓑ Ⓒ Ⓓ
47 Ⓐ Ⓑ Ⓒ Ⓓ 52 Ⓐ Ⓑ Ⓒ Ⓓ 57 Ⓐ Ⓑ Ⓒ Ⓓ 62 Ⓐ Ⓑ Ⓒ Ⓓ 66 Ⓐ Ⓑ Ⓒ Ⓓ 70 Ⓐ Ⓑ Ⓒ Ⓓ
48 Ⓐ Ⓑ Ⓒ Ⓓ 53 Ⓐ Ⓑ Ⓒ Ⓓ 58 Ⓐ Ⓑ Ⓒ Ⓓ

Word Recognition

71 Ⓐ Ⓑ Ⓒ Ⓓ 73 Ⓐ Ⓑ Ⓒ Ⓓ 75 Ⓐ Ⓑ Ⓒ Ⓓ 77 Ⓐ Ⓑ Ⓒ Ⓓ 79 Ⓐ Ⓑ Ⓒ Ⓓ 81 Ⓐ Ⓑ Ⓒ Ⓓ
72 Ⓐ Ⓑ Ⓒ Ⓓ 74 Ⓐ Ⓑ Ⓒ Ⓓ 76 Ⓐ Ⓑ Ⓒ Ⓓ 78 Ⓐ Ⓑ Ⓒ Ⓓ 80 Ⓐ Ⓑ Ⓒ Ⓓ

Contractions

82 Ⓐ Ⓑ Ⓒ Ⓓ 84 Ⓐ Ⓑ Ⓒ Ⓓ 85 Ⓐ Ⓑ Ⓒ Ⓓ 86 Ⓐ Ⓑ Ⓒ Ⓓ 87 Ⓐ Ⓑ Ⓒ Ⓓ 88 Ⓐ Ⓑ Ⓒ Ⓓ
83 Ⓐ Ⓑ Ⓒ Ⓓ

Spelling

89 Ⓐ Ⓑ Ⓒ Ⓓ 91 Ⓐ Ⓑ Ⓒ Ⓓ 92 Ⓐ Ⓑ Ⓒ Ⓓ 93 Ⓐ Ⓑ Ⓒ Ⓓ 94 Ⓐ Ⓑ Ⓒ Ⓓ 95 Ⓐ Ⓑ Ⓒ Ⓓ
90 Ⓐ Ⓑ Ⓒ Ⓓ

Root Words, Prefixes, and Suffixes

96 Ⓐ Ⓑ Ⓒ Ⓓ 98 Ⓐ Ⓑ Ⓒ Ⓓ 100 Ⓐ Ⓑ Ⓒ Ⓓ 102 Ⓐ Ⓑ Ⓒ Ⓓ 104 Ⓐ Ⓑ Ⓒ Ⓓ 105 Ⓐ Ⓑ Ⓒ Ⓓ
97 Ⓐ Ⓑ Ⓒ Ⓓ 99 Ⓐ Ⓑ Ⓒ Ⓓ 101 Ⓐ Ⓑ Ⓒ Ⓓ 103 Ⓐ Ⓑ Ⓒ Ⓓ

Capitalization

106 Ⓐ Ⓑ Ⓒ Ⓓ 107 Ⓐ Ⓑ Ⓒ Ⓓ 108 Ⓐ Ⓑ Ⓒ Ⓓ 109 Ⓐ Ⓑ Ⓒ Ⓓ 110 Ⓐ Ⓑ Ⓒ Ⓓ 111 Ⓐ Ⓑ Ⓒ Ⓓ

Punctuation

112 Ⓐ Ⓑ Ⓒ Ⓓ 113 Ⓐ Ⓑ Ⓒ Ⓓ 114 Ⓐ Ⓑ Ⓒ Ⓓ 115 Ⓐ Ⓑ Ⓒ Ⓓ

Parts of Speech

116 (A)(B)(C)(D) 118 (A)(B)(C)(D) 120 (A)(B)(C)(D) 122 (A)(B)(C)(D) 123 (A)(B)(C)(D) 124 (A)(B)(C)(D)
117 (A)(B)(C)(D) 119 (A)(B)(C)(D) 121 (A)(B)(C)(D)

Sentences

125 (A)(B)(C)(D) 126 (A)(B)(C)(D)

Main Idea

127 (A)(B)(C)(D) 128 (A)(B)(C)(D) 129 (A)(B)(C)(D) 130 (A)(B)(C)(D) 131 (A)(B)(C)(D) 132 (A)(B)(C)(D)

Sequence

133 (A)(B)(C)(D) 134 (A)(B)(C)(D) 135 (A)(B)(C)(D)

Characters and Settings

136 (A)(B)(C)(D) 137 (A)(B)(C)(D) 138 (A)(B)(C)(D) 139 (A)(B)(C)(D)

Predicting Outcomes

140 (A)(B)(C)(D) 141 (A)(B)(C)(D) 142 (A)(B)(C)(D) 143 (A)(B)(C)(D) 144 (A)(B)(C)(D)

Drawing Conclusions

145 (A)(B)(C)(D) 146 (A)(B)(C)(D) 147 (A)(B)(C)(D)

Cause and Effect

148 (A)(B)(C)(D) 149 (A)(B)(C)(D)

Fact versus Opinion

150 (A)(B)(C)(D) 151 (A)(B)(C)(D) 152 (A)(B)(C)(D) 153 (A)(B)(C)(D)

Reality versus Fantasy

154 (A)(B)(C)(D) 155 (A)(B)(C)(D)

Biography

156 (A)(B)(C)(D) 157 (A)(B)(C)(D) 158 (A)(B)(C)(D)

Poetry

159 (A)(B)(C)(D) 160 (A)(B)(C)(D) 161 (A)(B)(C)(D) 162 (A)(B)(C)(D)

Study Skills

163 (A)(B)(C)(D) 166 (A)(B)(C)(D) 169 (A)(B)(C)(D) 172 (A)(B)(C)(D) 175 (A)(B)(C)(D) 177 (A)(B)(C)(D)
164 (A)(B)(C)(D) 167 (A)(B)(C)(D) 170 (A)(B)(C)(D) 173 (A)(B)(C)(D) 176 (A)(B)(C)(D) 178 (A)(B)(C)(D)
165 (A)(B)(C)(D) 168 (A)(B)(C)(D) 171 (A)(B)(C)(D) 174 (A)(B)(C)(D)

VOCABULARY

Directions: Choose the correct word to go in the blank in these sentences.

1 Dad and Sarah went to the ____ to wash the clothes.

   (A) office

   (B) bedroom

   (C) garage

   (D) laundry

2 Sienna was afraid she had ___ her mittens.

   (A) found

   (B) lost

   (C) heard

   (D) sang

3 In the trees we heard a ____ sing.

   (A) squirrel

   (B) worm

   (C) bird

   (D) wolf

4 Bill was worried that his project was turning out to be a _____.

   (A) failure

   (B) success

   (C) good

   (D) treasure

STOP

PICTURE VOCABULARY

Directions: Look at each picture and choose the correct answer from the choices given below.

5 Which of the following pictures shows a child being angry?

Ⓐ

Ⓑ

Ⓒ

Ⓓ

6 Where is Tickle the rabbit playing?

Ⓐ in the flower bed

Ⓑ in the dog house

Ⓒ in the kitchen

Ⓓ in the trees

7 What is Jamal wearing?

Ⓐ a raincoat

Ⓑ jeans

Ⓒ shorts

Ⓓ swim trunks

GO

8 Which of these words tells what these dogs are doing?

(A) eating

(B) playing

(C) chasing cats

(D) sleeping

9 Which word tells what the child is doing?

(A) fighting

(B) eating

(C) running

(D) sleeping

STOP

WORDS IN CONTEXT

Directions: Read each sentence and choose the correct answer to fill in the blank.

10 All but the _____ children were able to reach the treats on the high shelf.

   Ⓐ tallest

   Ⓑ strongest

   Ⓒ shortest

   Ⓓ loudest

11 By the time dinner was served, we were very _____.

   Ⓐ angry

   Ⓑ silly

   Ⓒ young

   Ⓓ hungry

12 I was feeling _____ because my cat won first prize.

   Ⓐ sad

   Ⓑ tired

   Ⓒ happy

   Ⓓ silly

13 Cheryl's alarm did not ring, so she got to school _____.

   Ⓐ early

   Ⓑ alone

   Ⓒ sick

   Ⓓ late

14 At the store, Marcy took some money out of her _____.

   Ⓐ ribbon

   Ⓑ bureau

   Ⓒ purse

   Ⓓ bed

15 When Josh heard the _____ lion, he was scared.

   Ⓐ quiet

   Ⓑ gentle

   Ⓒ coughing

   Ⓓ roaring

16 The _____ soaked the lawn chairs.

Ⓐ moon

Ⓑ rain

Ⓒ wind

Ⓓ stars

17 After working in the stable for five hours, Rachel was _____.

Ⓐ tall

Ⓑ tired

Ⓒ laughing

Ⓓ tiny

Directions: Read each sentence and choose the answer that means the same as the underlined word.

18 Jose <u>smiled</u> when he saw his present.

Ⓐ grinned

Ⓑ sighed

Ⓒ yelled

Ⓓ cried

19 The snake's head moved very <u>quickly</u>.

Ⓐ happily

Ⓑ crookedly

Ⓒ slowly

Ⓓ fast

20 John was <u>satisfied</u> with his math test.

Ⓐ unhappy

Ⓑ sad

Ⓒ angry

Ⓓ content

21 Mom will <u>collect</u> our plates.

Ⓐ throw away

Ⓑ gather

Ⓒ hit

Ⓓ throw

22 Our school had <u>many</u> snow days.

Ⓐ several

Ⓑ lots of

Ⓒ limited

Ⓓ no

23 The girls <u>hopped</u> down the street.

Ⓐ walked

Ⓑ skipped

Ⓒ ran

Ⓓ slept

GO

Directions: Read the paragraph. Find the word below the paragraph that best fits in each numbered blank.

Charmaine and Elaine had a sleepover. First they filled the ___24___ with water and played with their toy ___25___. For dinner they cooked pizza in the ___26___. Then it was time to watch a ___27___ on TV. By the end of the long, busy day, they were very ___28___.

24 Ⓐ sink

    Ⓑ bed

    Ⓒ refrigerator

    Ⓓ counter

25 Ⓐ sand

    Ⓑ boats

    Ⓒ stones

    Ⓓ skates

26 Ⓐ refrigerator

    Ⓑ oven

    Ⓒ cupboard

    Ⓓ sink

27 Ⓐ chocolate

    Ⓑ video

    Ⓒ record

    Ⓓ seaweed

28 Ⓐ poor

    Ⓑ tired

    Ⓒ singing

    Ⓓ identical

STOP

SYNONYMS, ANTONYMNS, AND HOMONYMS

Directions: Look at the underlined word in each sentence. Which word is a **synonym** (a word that means the same thing) for the underlined word?

29 Sam looked at the book and didn't know where to <u>begin</u>.

- Ⓐ smile
- Ⓑ start
- Ⓒ stop
- Ⓓ run

30 Jason heard the wolf <u>howl</u>.

- Ⓐ cry
- Ⓑ laugh
- Ⓒ wash
- Ⓓ sniff

31 The <u>huge</u> tractor started plowing the field.

- Ⓐ small
- Ⓑ tiny
- Ⓒ large
- Ⓓ noisy

32 It's time to get some <u>sleep</u>.

- Ⓐ food
- Ⓑ rest
- Ⓒ dreams
- Ⓓ tired

Directions: Choose the pair of words below in which the words mean the same thing.

33 Ⓐ sleep wake
- Ⓑ listen talk
- Ⓒ walk stroll
- Ⓓ wide narrow

34 Ⓐ smile grin
- Ⓑ stand sit
- Ⓒ jumped ran
- Ⓓ slow fast

35 Ⓐ pat stroke
- Ⓑ hand fingers
- Ⓒ throw catch
- Ⓓ round square

GO ⇨

Directions: Look at the following sentences and pick the word that means the **opposite** of the word that is underlined.

36 We are going to a <u>big</u> parade.

   Ⓐ large

   Ⓑ tall

   Ⓒ small

   Ⓓ soft

37 Jim was <u>angry</u> when his friend broke his favorite model.

   Ⓐ angry

   Ⓑ happy

   Ⓒ surprised

   Ⓓ sad

38 I was to play <u>outside</u>.

   Ⓐ ball

   Ⓑ up

   Ⓒ inside

   Ⓓ tall

39 We were <u>wet</u> after the rain came.

   Ⓐ shivering

   Ⓑ hot

   Ⓒ cold

   Ⓓ dry

Directions: Read the following sentences and choose the correct word to fill in the blank.

40 The grass was wet with _____.

   Ⓐ do

   Ⓑ dew

   Ⓒ doe

   Ⓓ due

41 The bear had black _____.

   Ⓐ fir

   Ⓑ fur

   Ⓒ fer

   Ⓓ fire

42 The cat weighed five _____. He _____ the nails with a hammer.

   Ⓐ pine

   Ⓑ pins

   Ⓒ pounds

   Ⓓ ounces

43 The horse had a thick _____. I like to play _____ and seek.

   Ⓐ hair

   Ⓑ hide

   Ⓒ find

   Ⓓ mane

STOP

WORD SOUNDS

Directions: In which pair do the words **begin** with the same sound?

44 Ⓐ king   cane

    Ⓑ thin   tall

    Ⓒ cat   church

    Ⓓ ball   goat

45 Ⓐ dog   cat

    Ⓑ chart   cart

    Ⓒ giant   jewel

    Ⓓ cage   church

46 Ⓐ circus   cent

    Ⓑ call   say

    Ⓒ star   shine

    Ⓓ chin   can

47 Choose the word that has the same **beginning** sound as the word <u>bread</u>.

    Ⓐ pal

    Ⓑ bring

    Ⓒ ace

    Ⓓ pint

48 Choose the word with the same beginning sound as the word <u>cool</u>.

    Ⓐ step

    Ⓑ chimp

    Ⓒ kite

    Ⓓ get

Directions: Choose the letter that makes the **beginning** sound for each word pictured below.

49

    Ⓐ T

    Ⓑ S

    Ⓒ K

    Ⓓ Y

50

    Ⓐ C

    Ⓑ B

    Ⓒ S

    Ⓓ W

GO ⇒

51

- Ⓐ O
- Ⓑ S
- Ⓒ C
- Ⓓ T

52

- Ⓐ T
- Ⓑ S
- Ⓒ R
- Ⓓ E

Directions: Choose the word with the same **ending** sound as the underlined word in the question.

53 Which of these words has the same **ending** sound as the word <u>peach</u>?

- Ⓐ cat
- Ⓑ hiss
- Ⓒ path
- Ⓓ church

54 Which of these words has the same **ending** sound as the word <u>beach</u>?

- Ⓐ bunny
- Ⓑ reach
- Ⓒ ball
- Ⓓ hits

55 Which of these words has the same **ending** sound as the word <u>mass</u>?

- Ⓐ faith
- Ⓑ bass
- Ⓒ catch
- Ⓓ cat

56 Which of these words has the same **ending** sound as the word <u>seat</u>?

- Ⓐ star
- Ⓑ neat
- Ⓒ knees
- Ⓓ church

GO

Directions: Choose the letter that makes the ending sound for each word pictured below.

57

Ⓐ Q

Ⓑ C

Ⓒ L

Ⓓ T

58

Ⓐ M

Ⓑ B

Ⓒ N

Ⓓ K

59

Ⓐ J

Ⓑ G

Ⓒ D

Ⓓ S

Directions: Choose the letters that make the beginning sound for each word below.

60 shall

Ⓐ ch

Ⓑ s

Ⓒ sp

Ⓓ sh

61 slap

Ⓐ s

Ⓑ sp

Ⓒ st

Ⓓ sl

62 why

Ⓐ wh

Ⓑ w

Ⓒ we

Ⓓ h

63 grip

Ⓐ g

Ⓑ r

Ⓒ ge

Ⓓ gr

GO

Directions: Choose the letters that make the ending sound for each word below.

64 fist

- Ⓐ s
- Ⓑ sp
- Ⓒ st
- Ⓓ sl

65 disk

- Ⓐ ch
- Ⓑ ck
- Ⓒ i
- Ⓓ sk

66 first

- Ⓐ st
- Ⓑ s
- Ⓒ f
- Ⓓ sh

Directions: Match the word with the same vowel sound as the given word in each question.

67 What word has the same vowel sound as <u>hat</u>?

- Ⓐ cup
- Ⓑ chat
- Ⓒ head
- Ⓓ hip

68 What word has the same vowel sound as <u>bright</u>?

- Ⓐ star
- Ⓑ might
- Ⓒ coat
- Ⓓ fat

69 What word has the same vowel sound as <u>cook</u>?

- Ⓐ bring
- Ⓑ scat
- Ⓒ brook
- Ⓓ cake

70 What word has the same vowel sound as <u>team</u>?

- Ⓐ taught
- Ⓑ meet
- Ⓒ mat
- Ⓓ fight

STOP

WORD RECOGNITION

Directions: Choose the word that answers each of the following questions.

71 Which of these words means to cook bread?

   Ⓐ take

   Ⓑ mow

   Ⓒ bake

   Ⓓ iron

72 Which of these words means to travel in a car?

   Ⓐ ride

   Ⓑ shovel

   Ⓒ skate

   Ⓓ jump

73 Which of these words means to get clothes clean?

   Ⓐ dry

   Ⓑ iron

   Ⓒ wash

   Ⓓ dirty

74 Which of these words means to move through the air?

   Ⓐ swim

   Ⓑ fly

   Ⓒ fish

   Ⓓ boat

Directions: Choose the correct definition for each underlined word below.

75 Which of the definitions goes with the word <u>read</u>?

   Ⓐ put something into the stove

   Ⓑ clean the rugs

   Ⓒ use a book

   Ⓓ fry some eggs

76 Which of the definitions goes with the word <u>bed</u>?

   Ⓐ something that you can sleep in

   Ⓑ something you can put food into

   Ⓒ object that you drive

   Ⓓ underground thing that you can explore

77 Which of the definitions goes with the word <u>pen</u>?

   Ⓐ something you write with

   Ⓑ something you use to cook with

   Ⓒ something you use to hold two pieces of cloth together

   Ⓓ something you eat with

Directions: Choose the words below that are **compound words** (a word made up of two words).

78 Ⓐ foolish

   Ⓑ car

   Ⓒ streetcar

   Ⓓ hopping

79 Ⓐ scarecrow

   Ⓑ skated

   Ⓒ steam

   Ⓓ boat

80 Ⓐ fencepost

   Ⓑ hide

   Ⓒ playing

   Ⓓ sun

81 Ⓐ Halloween

   Ⓑ sleeping

   Ⓒ rainbow

   Ⓓ eat

STOP

CONTRACTIONS

Directions: Choose the words that were combined to make the following contractions.

82 couldn't

Ⓐ does not

Ⓑ did not

Ⓒ could not

Ⓓ doesn't

83 I'm

Ⓐ Im

Ⓑ I am

Ⓒ I was

Ⓓ I'm

84 didn't

Ⓐ didnt

Ⓑ didnt'

Ⓒ did not

Ⓓ would not

85 won't

Ⓐ would not

Ⓑ could not

Ⓒ will not

Ⓓ should not

86 wouldn't

Ⓐ would not

Ⓑ will not

Ⓒ should not

Ⓓ won't

87 What contraction means the same as <u>do not</u>?

Ⓐ doesn't

Ⓑ didn't

Ⓒ doe'snt

Ⓓ don't

88 What contraction means the same as <u>cannot</u>?

Ⓐ can't

Ⓑ couldn't

Ⓒ can'ot

Ⓓ cann't

SPELLING

Directions: Choose the correctly spelled word to go into the blank.

89 If something is not smooth, it is
____.

Ⓐ ruff

Ⓑ rauff

Ⓒ rough

Ⓓ roff

90 I do not want to ____ my cup.

Ⓐ brake

Ⓑ break

Ⓒ brak

Ⓓ brack

91 I fell ____.

Ⓐ dun

Ⓑ douwn

Ⓒ down

Ⓓ downe

92 I like to ___ up my clothes.

Ⓐ hang

Ⓑ han

Ⓒ hing

Ⓓ hange

93 Sam told us all a ___ funny joke.

Ⓐ relly

Ⓑ really

Ⓒ realy

Ⓓ rilly

94 Harry didn't ___ if he would go to the city tomorrow.

Ⓐ kno

Ⓑ know

Ⓒ knowe

Ⓓ no

95 ____ is the game I gave you?

Ⓐ Where

Ⓑ Wher

Ⓒ Whir

Ⓓ wher

STOP

ROOT WORDS, PREFIXES, AND SUFFIXES

Directions: What is the root word in the following underlined words?

96 <u>hardest</u>

Ⓐ harder

Ⓑ hard

Ⓒ hardest

Ⓓ est

97 <u>ugliest</u>

Ⓐ er

Ⓑ uglier

Ⓒ est

Ⓓ ugly

98 <u>shopping</u>

Ⓐ shop

Ⓑ shoppy

Ⓒ shoppin

Ⓓ shopping

99 <u>resting</u>

Ⓐ restier

Ⓑ rests

Ⓒ restin

Ⓓ rest

Directions: Identify the **suffix** in each of the following underlined words.

100 <u>batted</u>

Ⓐ bat

Ⓑ batt

Ⓒ ed

Ⓓ ba

101 <u>running</u>

Ⓐ ing

Ⓑ in

Ⓒ run

Ⓓ runnin

102 <u>sits</u>

Ⓐ s

Ⓑ its

Ⓒ sit

Ⓓ sits

Directions: Identify the **prefix** in each of the following underlined words.

103 <u>preorder</u>

 Ⓐ der

 Ⓑ er

 Ⓒ order

 Ⓓ pre

104 <u>undo</u>

 Ⓐ do

 Ⓑ un

 Ⓒ undo

 Ⓓ und

105 What does the prefix *re* mean in the word <u>rerun</u>?

 Ⓐ to run again

 Ⓑ to run for the first time

 Ⓒ to run after

 Ⓓ never to run

STOP

CAPITALIZATION

Directions: Read each sentence. Then choose the word that needs to begin with a capital letter.

106 she will bring me a present tomorrow.

   Ⓐ she

   Ⓑ will

   Ⓒ bring

   Ⓓ tomorrow

107 Antonio helped paul climb a tree.

   Ⓐ climb

   Ⓑ helped

   Ⓒ paul

   Ⓓ tree

108 The chorus will sing on sunday.

   Ⓐ chorus

   Ⓑ will

   Ⓒ sing

   Ⓓ sunday

109 i will go to the library.

   Ⓐ i

   Ⓑ will

   Ⓒ go

   Ⓓ library

Directions: Choose the sentence that shows correct capitalization.

110 Ⓐ I love to go to the Shore for vacation.

   Ⓑ I don't like Vanilla ice cream.

   Ⓒ Do you want to come to the theater with Shawn and me?

   Ⓓ Darlene is going to visit me in Northern New York.

111 Ⓐ Our little Dog is a Jack Russel Terrier.

   Ⓑ Tomorrow is Sunday, and we will go to church.

   Ⓒ At Noon we will have lunch.

   Ⓓ We like to carve pumpkins on halloween.

STOP

PUNCTUATION

Directions: Choose the sentence that shows correct punctuation.

112 Ⓐ I want you, to come!

Ⓑ Tomorrow we, can bring a cake?

Ⓒ Are you hungry?

Ⓓ What shall we do today.

113 Ⓐ How far is it to London?

Ⓑ Susan and Paul can, come to my house.

Ⓒ John, give this to her?

Ⓓ I want, you to go.

114 Ⓐ Bill Bob and I went to the store.

Ⓑ What kind of flower is that.

Ⓒ Mary, can you fly a kite!

Ⓓ Alex, will you be going to the party?

115 Ⓐ The flag is red white and blue.

Ⓑ Are you going to the fair?

Ⓒ Come and, take this to the teacher.

Ⓓ Jane please read the book?

STOP

PARTS OF SPEECH

Directions: Read the following sentences and choose the correct noun to go in the blank.

116 How many _____ were in the barn?

    Ⓐ cows

    Ⓑ cowz

    Ⓒ cow

    Ⓓ cows'

117 There were two ___ at the petting zoo.

    Ⓐ geeses

    Ⓑ goose

    Ⓒ gooses

    Ⓓ geese

Directions: Read the sentence and choose the letter underneath the word that is a noun.

118 Jill <u>took</u> <u>her</u> <u>cat</u> to <u>the</u> store.
    Ⓐ   Ⓑ   Ⓒ   Ⓓ

    Ⓐ took

    Ⓑ her

    Ⓒ cat

    Ⓓ the

Directions: Read the sentences below and choose the correct pronoun to go in the blank.

119 Jill threw ___ ball.

    Ⓐ she

    Ⓑ its

    Ⓒ her

    Ⓓ hers

120 I don't know if ____ will come with us.

    Ⓐ he

    Ⓑ him

    Ⓒ hers

    Ⓓ his

121 Kim likes horses. _____ likes horses.

    Ⓐ She

    Ⓑ Her

    Ⓒ He

    Ⓓ Him

GO ⇨

122 Patel and Betsy love to get dressed up. _____ love to get dressed up.

   Ⓐ Hers

   Ⓑ They

   Ⓒ Their

   Ⓓ She

123 There aren't any laces on _____ boots.

   Ⓐ hers

   Ⓑ him

   Ⓒ yours

   Ⓓ their

Directions: Choose the sentence that is written correctly.

124 Ⓐ She go to school.

   Ⓑ I like to work at school.

   Ⓒ Her dog like to run.

   Ⓓ Jeb, he went to school?

STOP

SENTENCES

Directions: Choose the sentence that is written correctly.

125 Ⓐ Sam took the ball.

Ⓑ Joe likes the pretty shirt green.

Ⓒ My tomorrow birthday is.

Ⓓ Going to the school you?

Directions: Read the two sentences. Choose the sentence that best combines the two sentences into one.

126 Cats like to hunt at night.
They hunt for mice.

Ⓐ Cats like to hunt at night for mice.

Ⓑ Cats like to hunt at night or hunt for mice.

Ⓒ Cats like to hunt at night but don't hunt for mice.

Ⓓ Cats like to hunt at night, hunt for mice.

STOP

MAIN IDEA

Directions: Read the following story and then answer the questions.

Clothes for Swimming

When people first started to swim in the 1800s, they wore swimsuits that looked like regular clothes. Women wore a dress to their knees. They also wore stockings and shoes. Men wore much the same thing. The clothes got so heavy it was hard to swim. In 1915 Carl Jantzen invented material that was comfortable to swim in.

127 What is this passage mostly about?

Ⓐ how to swim

Ⓑ when people started to swim

Ⓒ what swimmers wore in the 1800s

Ⓓ who Carl Jantzen was

128 What did women wear when they went swimming during the 1800s?

Ⓐ modern swimming suits

Ⓑ long pants

Ⓒ a dress, stockings, and shoes

Ⓓ an overcoat

129 What happened to change swimming clothes in 1915?

Ⓐ People stopped swimming.

Ⓑ People started wearing swim fins.

Ⓒ People wore heavier clothes.

Ⓓ Carl Jantzen invented a more comfortable swim outfit.

Ben Franklin

Benjamin Franklin proved that lightning was really electricity. He invented the lightning rod. He also invented bifocal glasses to help people see far away and close up at the same time. He invented the Franklin stove. He also started a post office, the first library in the United States, and the first fire department in Philadelphia.

130 What is the main idea of the passage?

Ⓐ Ben Franklin invented lots of useful things.

Ⓑ Lightning can cause fires.

Ⓒ Philadelphia needed a fire department.

Ⓓ Ben Franklin should have been president.

131 What did Ben Franklin find out about lightning?

Ⓐ It could hurt people.

Ⓑ It could burn things.

Ⓒ It was really electricity.

Ⓓ It could fly kites.

132 The passage says: "He invented bifocal glasses." What does bifocal mean in this sentence?

Ⓐ glasses that help people see in the dark

Ⓑ glasses that help people see far away and close up at the same time

Ⓒ glasses that help people see upside down

Ⓓ glasses for blind people

STOP

SEQUENCE

Directions: Read the passage. Choose the best answer to the following questions.

Tim decided he would paint a picture for his mother. Her birthday was the next day, and he wanted to give her something nice. His older sister Sandy had bought a present, but Tim liked to make his gifts. First, he got out his paper and watercolor box. Next, he went to the kitchen and filled a glass with water. He would need water to use his watercolor paints. Then he sketched a drawing with a pencil. Then he took his brush and filled in the outlines. Finally, he signed his picture. How surprised his mother would be!

133 What did Tim do first in the story?

   Ⓐ got water from the kitchen

   Ⓑ got out his paper and watercolor box

   Ⓒ started drawing an outline

   Ⓓ signed his name to the picture

134 Why did Tim want to paint a picture?

   Ⓐ It was his mother's birthday the next day.

   Ⓑ He wanted to share his painting at his school party.

   Ⓒ He liked to paint.

   Ⓓ He was bored.

135 How was Tim different from Sandy?

   Ⓐ He liked to buy his gifts.

   Ⓑ He liked to have other people buy his gifts.

   Ⓒ He was older than Sandy.

   Ⓓ He liked to make his gifts.

STOP

CHARACTERS AND SETTINGS

Directions: Read the passage. Choose the best answer to each question.

The New Baby

Paul walked slowly into the living room of his house. It was filled with people talking and laughing. They all crowded around his mother, who was holding his new baby brother. No one noticed Paul.

How he wished his baby brother had never been born! His mother and father used to spend the weekends doing lots of fun things with him. Now all they could talk about was his brother. Paul was worried that now that his little brother was here, his dad wouldn't have time for him anymore.

"Paul!" he heard his mother call. "Paul, come here!" He looked up and saw his mother smiling at him. She had handed his brother to Paul's grandmother. "Paul is the special guest here today," his mother told the crowd of visitors. "He's the big brother. It's his job to show the baby how to do lots of things. His brother will count on him to teach him lots of things, like how to throw a ball." Suddenly, Paul grinned and hugged his mother.

136 How does Paul feel at the start of the story?

Ⓐ happy about the new baby

Ⓑ tired from the new baby

Ⓒ confused about the new baby

Ⓓ upset about being ignored

137 Where does this story take place?

Ⓐ in Paul's house

Ⓑ in a classroom

Ⓒ in the cafeteria

Ⓓ in the gym

138 What is the location of this story like?

Ⓐ silent and empty

Ⓑ noisy and crowded

Ⓒ dark and scary

Ⓓ bright and hot

139 How does Paul probably feel when his mother calls to him?

Ⓐ angry

Ⓑ happy

Ⓒ lonesome

Ⓓ mad

PREDICTING OUTCOMES

Directions: Read the passage. Choose the best answer for the question that follows.

Story

Raw fish, called *sushi,* is popular in Japan. The people in Japan also eat beef cooked with noodles and vegetables, and fried fish and vegetables. Many of these dishes are also popular in the United States.

140 What is the best title for this passage?

Ⓐ Popular Japanese Food

Ⓑ What Is Sushi?

Ⓒ How to Fry Fish

Ⓓ What I Like to Eat

Directions: Choose the best answer for each question.

141 What is a book titled *Flopsy and Mopsy Bunny Paint Easter Eggs* most likely about?

Ⓐ a tale about two rabbits

Ⓑ a mystery involving secrets at Easter

Ⓒ two friends on a holiday

Ⓓ a sad story about a poor family

142 The best title for a book about all different kinds of animals that live in the ocean would be

Ⓐ *The Adventures of a Boy Fisherman.*

Ⓑ *Flying Fish and Me.*

Ⓒ *Wynken, Blynken, and Nod.*

Ⓓ *The Encyclopedia of Sea Creatures.*

Directions: Read the following passage and then choose the sentence that describes what would happen next.

First Jake took his pumpkin and scooped out the insides. Then he cut a face into it. Then he put a candle inside the pumpkin shell.

143 Ⓐ Jake lay down and went to sleep.

Ⓑ Jake threw the pumpkin at the trick or treaters.

Ⓒ Jake lit the candle in the pumpkin.

Ⓓ Jake went to put on his costume.

Directions: Read the following passage. Choose the statement that best describes what the story will probably be about.

It was dark outside. The wind howled in the trees, and some tree branches began to scratch against the window upstairs. Not a light glowed anywhere in the entire town.

144 Ⓐ The story will probably be about a scary mystery.

Ⓑ The story will probably be about something funny.

Ⓒ The story will probably be about happy children on a farm.

Ⓓ The story will probably be about weather.

STOP

DRAWING CONCLUSIONS

Directions: Read the following passage. Choose the best answer to each question.

Jill and Sarah were walking in the woods. They were gathering flowers. "Oh look!" Jill cried. "There is a little baby bear. Isn't he cute!" As she ran over to the bear, she heard something in the bushes. It was a very big bear!

"I think that's the mother," Sarah whispered.

145 What will probably happen next?

Ⓐ The girls will continue gathering flowers

Ⓑ Sarah and Jill will turn and run.

Ⓒ Sarah and Jill will offer some flowers to the mother bear.

Ⓓ Sarah and Jill will sit down and have lunch.

146 Who is Sarah?

Ⓐ Jill's aunt

Ⓑ Jill's mother

Ⓒ the bear

Ⓓ Jill's friend

Directions: Read the following passage and answer the question.

Mother sent Jared to his room for breaking his sister's toy. As Jared left, he said "I didn't do it!" Jim grinned as he saw Jared head to his room, and he thought to himself, "I got away with it."

147 Who broke his sister's toy?

Ⓐ Jared

Ⓑ Mom

Ⓒ his sister

Ⓓ Jim

STOP

CAUSE AND EFFECT

Directions: Read this passage and then answer the question.

Albert Einstein was a famous scientist. His ideas helped other scientists to make the first atom bomb. He also dreamed up many new ways of thinking about the world.

148 Albert Einstein was

    Ⓐ a young man.

    Ⓑ a brilliant scientist.

    Ⓒ running away to sea.

    Ⓓ friends with the king of England.

149 As a result of his inventions, other people made

    Ⓐ dinner.

    Ⓑ a new kind of telephone.

    Ⓒ electricity.

    Ⓓ the atom bomb.

STOP

FACT VERSUS OPINION

Directions: Read the following passage. Choose the best answer to each question.

Gliders Are Tops!

Jane Krantz is the country's top skater. She is only 12 but she beats everyone else in her class. Jane wears Gliders. She won't wear anything else. Gliders have extra-sharp blades that help people skate faster and better. Gliders come in beautiful gel colors. Gliders are the best!

150 Which idea from the passage is a fact?

 Ⓐ Jane Krantz is 12.

 Ⓑ Gliders are the best.

 Ⓒ Gliders are cool.

 Ⓓ You'll win if you wear Gliders.

151 Which idea from this passage is an opinion?

 Ⓐ Jane Krantz is the country's top skater.

 Ⓑ Jane beats everyone else in her class.

 Ⓒ Jane won't wear anything else.

 Ⓓ Gliders are the best.

152 The author's purpose in this passage is to

 Ⓐ talk about Jane's skating.

 Ⓑ teach you how to skate.

 Ⓒ convince you to buy Gliders.

 Ⓓ explain how skates are made.

Directions: Choose which of these sentences tells the writer's **opinion.**

The Billy Mine is run by bad people. They use ponies to pull heavy carts. The ponies have to live in the mine. They never see sunlight. They must work even when they are sick and tired. The ponies don't get enough to eat.

153 Ⓐ The mine ponies pull heavy carts.

 Ⓑ The ponies have to live in the mine.

 Ⓒ The ponies never see sunlight.

 Ⓓ The Billy Mine is run by bad people.

STOP

REALITY VERSUS FANTASY

Directions: Choose the correct answers for the following questions.

154 Which of these sentences is true?

(A) Humans have walked on Venus.

(B) There are people who live on Mars.

(C) Dinosaurs still walk the earth.

(D) Humans have explored the moon.

155 Which of these sentences is fantasy?

(A) Airplanes can fly through the air.

(B) Fairies live in flowers.

(C) Men can live in spaceships.

(D) Giant telescopes can peer far into space.

STOP

BIOGRAPHY

Directions: Read the following passage. Choose the correct answer to each question.

William Shakespeare

William Shakespeare was the greatest and most famous writer who ever lived. He lived almost 400 years ago in England. His plays are still enjoyed today. He wrote stories about love, like *Romeo and Juliet*. He also wrote plays about history.

156 William Shakespeare was

   Ⓐ the first African-American in space.

   Ⓑ the most famous writer who ever lived.

   Ⓒ an English king.

   Ⓓ an actor.

157 One of Shakespeare's plays was

   Ⓐ *Romeo and Juliet.*

   Ⓑ *Cats.*

   Ⓒ *The Wizard of Oz.*

   Ⓓ *Alice in Wonderland.*

Mother Teresa

Mother Teresa was a Roman Catholic nun. She won the Nobel Peace Prize in 1979. She spent her life trying to help the world's poor and hungry. She was born in Yugoslavia in 1910 and went to India in 1930. She worked among the poor in Calcutta. She founded a group of nuns who helped her.

158 Mother Teresa is remembered as

   Ⓐ a nun who helped the poor.

   Ⓑ a great queen.

   Ⓒ a good doctor.

   Ⓓ an Indian ruler.

STOP

POETRY

Directions: Read the poem excerpt. Answer the following questions about the poem.

The Night Before Christmas
By Clement Moore

'Twas the night before Christmas, when all through the house

Not a creature was stirring, not even a mouse;

The stockings were hung by the chimney with care,

In hopes that St. Nicholas soon would be there;

The children were nestled all snug in their beds,

While visions of sugar-plums danced in their heads;

And mamma in her 'kerchief, and I in my cap,

Had just settled down for a long winter's nap,

159 From this poem, you can tell that

   Ⓐ it's Christmas Eve.

   Ⓑ it is cold.

   Ⓒ the author doesn't like to sleep.

   Ⓓ it's the author's birthday.

160 What does the title tell us about the poem?

   Ⓐ Children like to sleep.

   Ⓑ It will be describing what happens on the night before Christmas.

   Ⓒ The moon is the main topic.

   Ⓓ There are a lot of elves and magical creatures around.

161 What does it mean that "visions of sugar-plums danced in their heads"?

   Ⓐ The children went to bed hungry.

   Ⓑ The children were dreaming about Christmas treats.

   Ⓒ The children were sick.

   Ⓓ The children were arguing.

162 Who is St. Nicholas?

   Ⓐ another name for the Easter Bunny

   Ⓑ the children's grandfather

   Ⓒ Santa Claus

   Ⓓ the local fireman

STUDY SKILLS

Directions: In the following list of alphabetical words, choose the word that comes next in correct alphabetical order from the choices below.

163 ate   ear   sat

    Ⓐ corn

    Ⓑ want

    Ⓒ dig

    Ⓓ rub

164 bear   been   bop

    Ⓐ bean

    Ⓑ bus

    Ⓒ biscuit

    Ⓓ born

165 baby   bad   bask

    Ⓐ bat

    Ⓑ bear

    Ⓒ bare

    Ⓓ bar

Directions: Read the following questions and choose the correct answer for each.

166 Which word would you find on the following dictionary page, between the guide words *cat* and *cot*?

cat	cot

    Ⓐ cub

    Ⓑ crab

    Ⓒ cut

    Ⓓ caw

167 Which word would you **not** find on the dictionary page above?

    Ⓐ creep

    Ⓑ catamount

    Ⓒ cobblestone

    Ⓓ corn

bat	bend

168 What word would you find on the dictionary page above?

Ⓐ bun

Ⓑ bent

Ⓒ burp

Ⓓ beat

169 What word would you **not** find on the dictionary page above?

Ⓐ bunny

Ⓑ beat

Ⓒ bawl

Ⓓ bee

170 If you wanted to find out how to pronounce the word *glitch,* where would you look?

Ⓐ atlas

Ⓑ encyclopedia

Ⓒ dictionary

Ⓓ newspaper

171 What things could you **not** find in an atlas?

Ⓐ how to pronounce a word

Ⓑ where a city is located

Ⓒ where a country is found

Ⓓ what is north of a state

Directions: Look at the graph below. Choose the correct answer to each question.

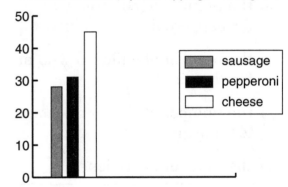

Number of favorite pizza toppings in our grade

172 What does the white bar represent?

Ⓐ the number of children who prefer cheese

Ⓑ the number of children who prefer pepperoni

Ⓒ the number of children who prefer sausage

Ⓓ the number of students

173 What does the black bar represent?

- Ⓐ the number of children who prefer pepperoni
- Ⓑ the number of children who prefer cheese
- Ⓒ the number of children who prefer sausage
- Ⓓ the number of students

174 What does the gray bar represent?

- Ⓐ the number of children who prefer pepperoni
- Ⓑ the number of children who prefer cheese
- Ⓒ the number of children who prefer sausage
- Ⓓ the number of students

175 How many children prefer cheese?

- Ⓐ about 30
- Ⓑ about 10
- Ⓒ about 45
- Ⓓ none

Directions: Choose the correct answer for the following questions.

176 If Susan wanted to find in a book a specific page that discussed diseases of dalmation dogs, where would she look?

- Ⓐ glossary
- Ⓑ table of contents
- Ⓒ title page
- Ⓓ index

177 As you read a book about the planets, you come to a word you don't understand. Where would you find a definition of this word?

- Ⓐ table of contents
- Ⓑ glossary
- Ⓒ index
- Ⓓ title page

178 Tim wants to get a general idea of the topics covered in his book. He would look in

- Ⓐ the table of contents.
- Ⓑ the glossary.
- Ⓒ the index.
- Ⓓ the title page.

STOP

Answer Key
for Sample Practice Test

Vocabulary

1	D
2	B
3	C
4	A

Picture Vocabulary

5	B
6	A
7	D
8	B
9	C

Words in Context

10	C
11	D
12	C
13	D
14	C
15	D
16	B
17	B
18	A
19	D
20	D
21	B
22	B
23	B
24	A
25	B

26	B
27	B
28	B

Synonyms, Antonyms, and Homonyms

29	B
30	A
31	C
32	B
33	C
34	A
35	A
36	C
37	B
38	C
39	D
40	B
41	B
42	C
43	B

Word Sounds

44	A
45	C
46	A
47	B
48	C
49	C

50	B
51	C
52	A
53	D
54	B
55	B
56	B
57	D
58	A
59	B
60	D
61	D
62	A
63	D
64	C
65	D
66	A
67	B
68	B
69	C
70	B

Word Recognition

71	C
72	A
73	C
74	B
75	C
76	A
77	A

78	C
79	A
80	A
81	C

Contractions

82	C
83	B
84	C
85	C
86	A
87	D
88	A

Spelling

89	C
90	B
91	C
92	A
93	B
94	B
95	A

Root Words, Prefixes, and Suffixes

96	B
97	D
98	A
99	D

100	C
101	A
102	A
103	D
104	B
105	A

Capitalization

106	A
107	C
108	D
109	A
110	C
111	B

Punctuation

112	C
113	A
114	D
115	B

Parts of Speech

116	A
117	D
118	C
119	C
120	A
121	A

122	B
123	D
124	B

Sentences

125	A
126	A

Main Idea

127	C
128	C
129	D
130	A
131	C
132	B

Sequence

133	B
134	A
135	D

Characters and Settings

136	D
137	A
138	B
139	B

Predicting Outcomes

140	A
141	A
142	D
143	C
144	A

Drawing Conclusions

145	B
146	D
147	D

Cause and Effect

148	B
149	D

Fact versus Opinion

150	A
151	D
152	C
153	D

Reality versus Fantasy

154	D
155	B

Biography

156	B
157	A
158	A

Poetry

159	A
160	B
161	B
162	C

Study Skills

163	B
164	D
165	A
166	D
167	A
168	D
169	A
170	C
171	A
172	A
173	A
174	C
175	C
176	D
177	B
178	A

DATE DUE

OCT 1 9 2005			
OCT 1 9 REC'D			
GAYLORD			PRINTED IN U.S.A.